Soulful freedom®
Sacred Journey to Authenticity

MaryLou Hunter, HHP

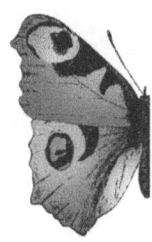

Copyright © 2013 by MaryLou Hunter, HHP
First Edition

All rights reserved. No part of this book shall be reproduced, stored in a retrieval system, or transmitted by any means without written permission from the author.

ISBN 978-0-9883438-2-5

Printed in the United States of America
Instantpublisher.com

Printed in the United States of America
CreativeSpace.com

dedication

*This book is dedicated to you.
I encourage you to allow yourself
to experience Soulful Freedom®.*

acknowledgements

There are so many people in my life that I am grateful for but when I look back and reflect on this journey I offer gratitude to:

Mom, thank you for your love and friendship in my life. You were my anchor when I needed grounding.

Sabrena, Janet, Dino and Vera Jo, thank you for being there through my darkest moments and still encouraging and loving me unconditionally. Thank you for accepting the life changing decisions I have made for my life and not judging me!

Erika, all of our talks over wine has encouraged me to move forward in accomplishing my dreams. Thank you for your friendship.

My healing sisters; Maya, Donna, Melinda, Audra, Alice, Keri, Ali B., Sheila, Marie, Maren, Bel and Valerie, thank you for teaching me the importance of true sisterhood. Working with you has been very healing and the bond we created was, and still is, such a sacred bond. Every single one of you were my healing angels and helped me in the most pivotal time in my life.

Joey, my Spirit Sister, thank you for taking me back home to my Shaman roots. Your timing in my life was Divine. Your guidance and friendship has been such a blessing.

Marla, your gentle touch helped me get through all the edits. You are the glue of this book. I thank you from the bottom of my heart.

My Clients, your support has been such a blessing in my life. Each one of you are my unique miracles of inspiration. Because of each of you, I am very blessed.

A special thank you to...
John, you have been the perfect parent; always loving and accepting me for who I am. You have been my hero because of your unconditional love and guidance in my life.

Kiana, you're a sweet spirit who is quite often my inspiration. Your unconditional love is my daily reminder to live in a high vibration. I am blessed you are in my life.

Danielle, you are my most precious gift. You have been my daily motivator and joy. You are always supporting me and encouraging me to be happy. Not only am I blessed you are my daughter, but truly blessed we have such a special relationship.

Stacey, you are my love, my life, my beautiful Soul Mate. Thank you for being my best friend and not allowing me to accept mediocrity. You continue to challenge me to get out of my comfort zone and be my best. Your love, devotion and loyalty to me has been my rock; loving and accepting who I am and having you to love makes me feel perfect in my skin. I am so blessed you are in my life!

Disclaimer
I wrote this book to support you in finding your Soulful Freedom. The suggestions, therapeutic process and nutrition advice described in this book are no way meant to replace medical or mental advice from your doctor. Please consult your doctor if you have any questions. In addition, while this book offers rituals or ceremonies that are healing, this book does not replace formal instruction from your medical doctor.

1	A Listing of Mantras	
3	Forward	
5	How to Use this Book	
7	Preface	
15	Chapter One	**Strip the Barnacles**
2	Chapter Two	**Reaffirm Your Values**
31	Chapter Three	**Restructure Your Beliefs**
37	Chapter Four	**Attack Your Fear(s)**
47	Chapter Five	**Change Your Rules**
53	Chapter Six	**Let Go of the Old You**
61	Chapter Seven	**Define the New You**
71	Chapter Eight	**Treat Every Day as if it is the Last Day of Your Life**
79	Chapter Nine	**Embrace Your New Spirituality**
93	Chapter Ten	**Learn to Live in a Higher Vibration**
111	Chapter Eleven	**Live Your Virtue's Honestly**
119	Chapter Twelve	**Take Care of Your Temple**
129	Chapter Thirteen	**Become the New You**
135		**About the Author**

21	Unique Soul
30	Self-value
36	I Believe
46	Courage
51	My Rules
59	I Am Perfect
68	Soul Freedom
77	Positive Vibration
91	In the Light
110	Self-honor
117	I Am Blessed
127	Organic Love
133	I Am

forward

My own journey has been a very public one from Victim to Thriver, and like MaryLou my quest has been to help others to live the most profound, authentic, and peaceful lives possible. It has been my privilege these 22 years to watch MaryLou fulfill her life's purpose.

I first knew her as a student in my communication class in 1991. Since then I have witnessed her desire and passion for knowledge as she became a wellness coach and relationship expert. She exudes vitality and energy as she works compassionately to help people in their own healing journey.

She has conquered many obstacles in life, and because of that she is well equipped to help others. Her book will help you to develop the confidence and courage to discover the authentic you. I describe her works/wellness coaching as dynamic, intelligent, creative, inspirational and real. It is a privilege and pleasure to support her works and challenge each reader to allow Soulful Freedom® into their personal and spiritual life.

Her book, *Soulful Freedom*® is an eye opening concept that is needed in the Western World. She brilliantly describes the value in creating a personal structure that helps bridge the gap when someone is not authentic with their beliefs. Her views on Spirituality are profound, and embrace the true essence of spiritual equality.

Donna Friess, Ph.D
Life Coach, Relationship and Grief Expert
Author of *Cry the Darkness: One Woman's Triumph Over the Tragedy of Incest*, HCI, 1993

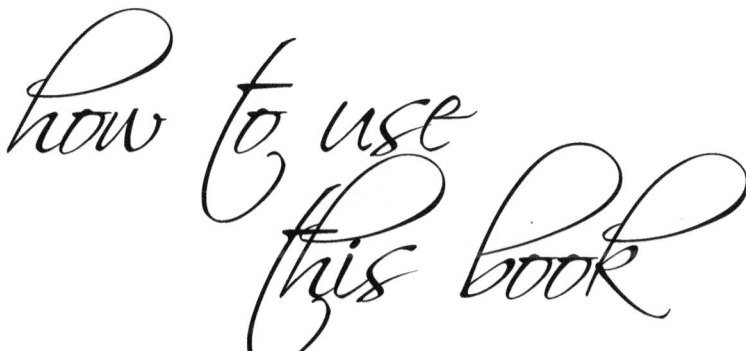
how to use this book

- Allow this book to be your guide to find Soulful Freedom.
- The purpose of this book is to take you out of your comfort zone and challenge you to live your life authentically.
- This book is meant to be read from beginning to end... many times.
- I encourage you to give this book to someone else to read.
- Don't focus on typing mistakes or misspelled words. I encourage you to read with an open heart and celebrate You because this book is for You.
- Commit to reading the entire book.

Throughout your journey to have Soulful Freedom® I encourage you to visit my website www.marylouhunter.com to check out my latest tools and resources. You will find information about my latest workshops, services and teleseminars. You will also find many articles I have written that are helpful in your healing journey. Remember, I am here to help you when you need it. I look forward to talking to you and helping you with your healing journey.

- MaryLou

preface

I was born in Hot Springs, Arkansas and was raised on 80 acres that my Mamah owned. She lived in a two-bedroom home with an old barn. There was an old well in the back of the house that still had water. I know because I loved picking up acorns off the ground and throwing them into the well to hear the hollow sound when the acorn hit the water. Mamah and Uncle Tom built a pantry house about 100 yards from the back porch where they stored their canned jelly and vegetables. About a quarter mile down the road my mom and dad lived in a smaller two-bedroom home where five of us kids slept in one room. Other than the few years my dad moved us to California for work, this is where I lived in my early years.

My Uncle Tom and Mamah raised a few cows and pigs for food. They also plowed a garden and I remember helping pick the vegetables. I loved watching Mamah and Mom making jelly and canning Purple Hull Peas, while listening to their stories and enjoying them singing their way through a long day. The kitchen table was our circle where we told stories, played dice, dominos, card games, and ate plenty of food. I honestly believe that sitting around that kitchen table was one of my most favorite childhood memories.

My childhood was a simple one. I have wonderful memories of playing outside. I got so excited when Mamah gave each of us kids a bowl, telling us to go out in the field and pick wild blackberries for cobbler that night. On our way, we chased cows and ran for our lives because they got tired of being harassed and charged at us.

Besides chasing cows, my biggest thrill was hanging out in the old barn and climbing up the ladder hoping I would not fall through the rotten wood. When I got to the top of the loft in the barn, the drop seemed so high and it always took me a few minutes to get the courage to jump. Beside the barn was some sort of tree that had these huge bean pods dangling from it. When they dried out, my two older sisters smoked them, making me take a puff so I wouldn't tell on them.

On the hot summer days we ate yellow-meated watermelon and then piled up in the back of Uncle Tom's pickup and drove to the local creek to cool off. I never had a ton of material things, but I always had good food, love, laughter, and my family.

On Saturdays the local Baptist church bus came by to check to see how many of us kids were going to church the next day. Mom always tried to get rid of us kids so that she could have some peace and quiet time. I was always ready to catch the bus because I loved the glazed donuts they gave to us as a treat for going to church. My Mom and Mamah never went to church. They were not religious but more Native American in their beliefs. My great grandma was full blood Cherokee which makes me an eighth.

My mom and dad lived a very simple life with little education and a big family. They did all they could just to get by. I truly believe they were amazing and did the best they could with what they had. My mom and dad divorced when I was 11, and that started the beginning of a whole new lifestyle.

When my mom married my step dad, my entire life changed. He remodeled our house and added two more bedrooms, a bathroom, and a den with a huge fireplace. I think that was the same year the city paved the dirt road which led to our house. One of the first summers my mom and step dad were married, his four kids came to visit for the entire summer. My mom had nine kids in the house.

And when my Dad married my step mom she already had three kids; later on, they had one together. I guess the universe thought four siblings was not enough for me and gave me eight more. My life at the very least was not boring. I loved the excitement of all the new changes; the feeling of belonging to and being part of something big. I always felt the need to be right in the middle of it all.

My step dad traveled with his job and after a few years, he moved us to Houston, Texas where we lived for four years. Our first 'house' was a two-story apartment and my bedroom window overlooked the courtyard where at first I would just sit for hours and watch all the kids hanging out. It was a little scary for me because I had only hung around my siblings for the most part.

My first job was at Noble Romans Pizza. I would walk back and forth to work, and one night I didn't get home till 2 in the morning because we talked the manager into letting us drink beer after closing. I knew I was in trouble when I walked through the front door and mom was in her rocking chair just waiting for me. I was pretty drunk and don't even remember walking home. I was only 14, and that night was the beginning of my rebellion and hanging with the wrong crowd. I started drinking and smoking pot because I thought it was the cool thing to do. Looking back, I never felt like I belonged when we lived in the apartments. It never felt like home.

My younger brother, sister and I spent summers with my Dad and step mom in Southern California. I loved visiting my new family and getting to know my new sisters. On weekends, we would pile into the car for day trips to Disneyland and Knott's Berry Farm. I enjoyed having picnics at the park because we were all together as a family. We played horseshoes and ate all day. Our picnics at the beach included a bonfire and we always roasted hotdogs and made S'mores. The summers with my Dad were a blast and I always loved being part of his new family. It was exciting and it seemed like a new adventure every day.

The summer after eighth grade I came back from Southern California to our new home in Texas. My mom and step dad spent the summer moving from the apartments into our new home. It was the first time I had my own room. Life was good and I felt very rich, and most importantly, I didn't feel lost like I did in the apartments. I felt like I belonged again.

Just after I finished 11th grade, my step dad came home and told us we were moving again. We went from Arkansas, to Texas and now to Waterloo, Belgium. Wow, talk about a culture shock! As soon as we landed I realized I was way out of my comfort zone, yet really excited to embark on this new adventure. I can remember being so worried that I would not fit in.

We lived in a hotel for what seemed like several months, but probably only a few weeks. I woke up to the smell of fresh coffee and croissants every day. The food was very different than what I was used to; fried potatoes, beans and corn bread. The restaurants did not put ice in the soda nor was there a local liquor store that sold Dr. Pepper, Twinkies and Doritos. We ate a ton of breads, cheese and sausage. The pastries were so good, and I had no problem adjusting to the new types of food.

During our stay in the hotel, I met a group of kids my age that were kids of Assembly of God ministries, where I wasted no time in finding my new boyfriend. I adjusted fast and loved the new changes.

Back home in Arkansas, I grew up on Old Bear Road and I remember driving up to our new home and glancing down at my new Belgium ID with my new address; avenue de la Belgerie. I was in shock when I saw our new home. It was a surreal moment, and for the first time in my life I did not feel like a poor hillbilly living on Old Bear Road. My step dad parked the car and I looked up at what seemed to be a mansion. We walked into the front door and there was a marble foyer with a marble staircase to the upstairs bedrooms. My room was bigger than my Texas room and I had my very own sink. Yes, in my room! The top floor had five rooms and my mom made the fifth room her sewing room. There was a bathroom that had a bidet. My mom didn't know what a bidet was, so she stuck a fern in it and it became a plant stand until one of my dad's coworkers came over for dinner and needed to use it. Still to this day, we laugh about that story. Downstairs had a huge kitchen, formal dining room, family room and my dad's office, and of course don't forget the marble foyer. The bottom floor was your typical basement where mom did laundry and dad tinkered. My European adventure was a time for rebirth. I became a born again Christian and was very zealous with my beliefs. I graduated high school in Europe and moved to California to start my life as an adult.

When I moved to California, all I wanted was to find happiness and have a love life as my mom and step dad had. Also, I wanted to be the perfect Christian witness. After a few years I met the man I married. He was Jewish, but I knew that my God was better and that I could convert him so that he could get saved. We were married for 18 years and had a beautiful daughter who became the center of my life.

In my daughter's infant and toddler years I was heavily involved in church. This kept me very busy and made me feel needed. I was so involved in church, I decided to become a Gospel Clown, so I took a trip to Colorado with my daughter and graduated from clown school. Then I became the children's church pastor and the gospel clown of my church. My husband was never involved with my church activities, nor did he ever convert. Looking back, we didn't do much together as a couple.

Once my daughter started pre-school, I became bored and decided to go to college and become a Psychologist. I wanted to save the world; little did I know that in order to do that, I had to become authentic with me. I started realizing how much I had masked my true feelings about love, life and God. I had no idea I was living in denial.

After four years of majoring in Psychology I started feeling depressed. My body ached to the point where I could not get out of bed. I had no energy and spent my days just lying around the house and sometimes not even getting out of bed. This was hard for me, because I was always on the go; to suddenly not have the energy to take my daughter to school was overwhelming and frightening.

When I went to the doctor, the first doctor told me that my pain was in my head and he told me I needed to seek therapy. The second doctor took my blood work, and when the results came in, told me that I had Chronic Fatigue and said I would have to live a stress-free life and prescribed anti-depressant pills.

Those pills made me sick and I felt like I was not even in my body. I seemed worse off than before; still did not have energy, and to top it off, I was spacey. After almost a decade, which I call my dark ages, I hit rock bottom.

I was physically sick and mentally unstable. I felt lost, lonely, depressed and confused. I was living at the opposite end of my dreams. I was the perfect example of a typical Pollyanna housewife, who on the outside seemed perfect, but on the inside was slowly dying. I was so angry that my life did not turn out the way I planned. I had been living my life as a lie and no one knew my dark secrets of pain. How could I tell the world that I have everything that I thought I wanted and needed and yet, I was miserable? I kept asking myself "How did I get here? Where did I go wrong? Why am I the only one in pain? I had an amazing life so what is wrong with me?"

At this point I knew I needed to drastically change my life. It was important both for my health and for the health of my daughter. Looking back, when I first started my healing journey almost a decade and a half ago, I became what I call "organically born again" and on a journey that I called "Soulful Freedom". I am now living a life where I feel very comfortable in my skin. I have finally found my real peace and spiritual empowerment.

The reason why I was sick is because I was my own road block. I was not authentic with my life, values and beliefs. I was only authentic with what I wanted to believe. Looking back, I take full responsibility for my journey, my transformations, and especially, the road blocks I encountered. It was my journey and I had to find my way and not live life someone else's way.

It doesn't matter what your story is, the important thing is where do you go from where you don't want to be? How do you free yourself from everything that holds you hostage? How do you get comfortable in your skin? How can you experience Soulful Freedom?

If you are ready to experience Soulful Freedom®, let's begin.

Chapter One
strip the barnacles

Unique Soul

Even though I had an amazing childhood, I did not realize that I internalized and adopted all the labels that were given to me. Now before I continue, let me make it clear that I do not blame anyone for labeling me. To be honest, I don't remember where some of the labels even came from. I also take full responsibility in holding on tight and not letting go. I always had a choice to accept or reject any thoughts or opinions that someone else had of me. It just took me a long time to realize it.

These are some of the labels/remarks I remember...
- You are a beautiful girl
- You are the oddball of the bunch
- Good thing you are cute because you are not that smart
- Hopefully you will find a good man to take care of you
- You are a sweet soul
- You are in your own world
- Earth to MaryLou
- Mom must have had an affair with Mr. Kellogg because you are a Fruit Loop
- It will be a miracle if you finish high school
- Your good looks will get you far

Because I internalized these labels, I did not find at first the person I would call my soul mate. I found a good man that would take care of me. I had everything I wanted. He was nine years older than me. He had a great personality and good work habits. He was educated and I knew that I would have the life that I wanted and deserved. I was a kept woman and in my mind it was a good thing because I did what I was told, "Hopefully you will find a good man to take care of you". Unfortunately holding on to that belief made me lonely and miserable.

When I started realizing that my labels/beliefs were holding me back, I knew that I had to change and reframe my thoughts. All of these labels I was carrying needed to be reassessed and redefined. Through the years I stripped one barnacle off at a time with this formula from my critical thinking class.

1. *Is it true?*
2. *Do I accept or reject it?*
3. *What do I do to change the feeling?*

I always felt beautiful and knew that I had a good heart so I decided to accept being beautiful and having a sweet soul. The challenge was to be beautiful and smart. For so long I accepted that I was not smart enough, and it is a dark shadow still to be reckoned with. But every day I ask myself,

Is it true?

No, and I continue to educate myself. I actually am grateful to have been accused of not being smart, just to prove everyone wrong. The irony is I have the highest degree of education among my siblings. What did I do to change the feeling? I used the label as fuel to fill my soul with all the knowledge that I needed to sustain me. It was a hard barnacle to strip, but in the end I accepted that fact that I am good enough and worthy of my education. I accepted the fact that there are many people smarter than I, and many that are not. I am perfect and right on time in my universe.

Being called a Fruit Loop or odd was not healthy for me growing up. I wanted so much to be like everyone else. I wanted to be accepted as normal and I wanted to be part of the in-crowd. I tried so hard to fit in and I actually carried that label up until seven years ago. Oddly enough this label did not need to be stripped, just redefined.

I remember when I was nine, picking up rocks in my front yard and feeling the different temperature and vibrations from each rock. I still have a few of those rocks in my jewelry box because I believed they would help heal my surroundings and be of good luck in my life.

I used to spend hours walking through our 80 acres and feeling different air densities and pockets of hollow energy. I even felt like I was being watched when I knew someone was not there.

I was a big daydreamer. I would find myself journeying to places I had never been before. I talked to trees, cows, even the clouds in the sky. When I touched someone, especially older people, I could feel their goodness or darkness. Even when I seemed to be alone in a room, I could always sense the presence of another, dead or alive.

I always felt energy come out of my hands and I even remember casting my hand out in the air, sending energy to heal the world. All my life, my stomach would tighten if I was around someone that needed healing and it would only loosen up when I said a protective prayer for that person and send good blessings. Still today, this is true.

I was always trying to find my way so I would be either on one end of the fence or the other, never in the middle. And when I believed in something I was 110% passionate. My embrace on life allowed me to be in my own little world.

What I realized is that I am more intuitive than some. All of those sensations I experienced as the "odd ball" child, and even into my adult years, have been the Universe teaching me the things I needed to know for my mission in life, which is to balance energy in one through healing the mind, body and soul.

What the healing link to this belief is, that being odd, being different, being called Fruit Loop was only negative because I believed it so. I could have just as easily believed that I was special. But for years, I allowed myself to believe that being odd was not good enough. This baggage was mine and I carried it on many trips. The good news is that I still carry it. It has a new shape, new meaning and a new color. It's my favorite luggage.

It doesn't matter what your label is, you are told many things growing up. What matters is what you believe and what you are going to do with the information.

When you change your emotional state about the label, you can begin to see your life as ways to:
- *Create opportunities*
- *Make your weakness a strength*
- *Make the impossible possible*
- *Understand that unkindness is a lack of understanding*
- *Experience soulful freedom*

Unique Soul Mantra

I am a unique soul
that is perfect in the light of my Universe.
I am worthy of my thoughts, wants, needs and desires.
I trust in myself to take responsibility
over my emotions and feelings.
I take responsibility in my temple
and I will protect it like no one else can.
I have authority over me
and I hold the key to what comes in or goes out.
I am strong and I have courage to accomplish all things.

Chapter Two
reaffirm your values

Self-value

The first seven years of our life we collect values from our environment and experiences. As you evolve, so do your values. We define our values, we choose them, and we allow them to alter our life.

Aside from the values of love, peace, family, harmony and happiness that many people share, I also valued belonging, acceptance and affection the most while growing up.

As a child I needed to be the center of attention. I was always in the middle of everyone trying to get something out of someone. I craved affection and was very lovable because of it. I was one of those clinging kids that would sit in your lap, comb your hair, tickle your back and not leave your side. It was important for me to be accepted in all social groups in school because I had to be liked by everyone. I truly needed to belong.

As an adult, I found myself giving more than I wanted just to be liked or needed. If I was not the center of all happiness and love in everyone's life, I felt unbalanced and unwanted.

When I took a Conflict Resolution class in college, one of my homework assignments was to write a journal of all my family conflicts. My professor took time out with each student in private to review their work. Her words to me were so profound. She asked me why I needed to be involved in every aspect of my family's life; at the time I could not answer her. Her lecture that day was about taking responsibility for all your conflicts and that you are the root cause of all your conflicts.

A few years later I thought of her words in that very lecture and realized I was in conflict with myself and that I needed to change my values in order to move forward in my healing process.

Everything I had valued and held close to my heart was burning a hole in my soul. It felt like I went to bed as a size seven and woke up the next morning in a size 12. My skin was no longer comfortable needing affection, acceptance or a sense of belonging at the expense of my own wants, needs and desires.

Realization was the easiest part. The time it took me to get from point A to point B was much harder. I had to learn that sacrificing my values for new ones might cause my life a few trimmers, mostly internal.

My values as a child and young adult ruled my life, which then set the stage for everything that went on around me. My thoughts and feelings became my actions which affected my results: my wants, needs and desires. When I became aware that I outgrew my values, I was motivated to change and started moving towards my new goals.

In a later chapter you will understand my fear of sacrifice and how it ties into my healing process.

This exercise will help you find your core values. When was the last time you took a good look at your core values?

Take a look at the list on the next three pages.
- Circle 30 values that apply to you
- Out of that 30, reduce it to 15
- Out of the 15, pick your top 7

Ask yourself these three questions?
1. Are you living your life according to your values?
2. Are your values allowing you to accomplish your wants, needs and desires?
3. Are your values being manifested in your personal, spiritual and professional life?

If you have answered "No" to any of these questions you might need to re-evaluate your values. Walking in authenticity is a key element to healing. Your body will start to break down on all levels if you are not congruent. Be truthful, you owe it to yourself to become transparent.

My Core Values

a
abundance
acceptance
accomplishment
accuracy
achievement
acknowledgement
activeness
adaptability
adoration
adroitness
adventure
affection
affluence
aggressiveness
agility
alertness
altruism
ambition
amusement
anticipation
appreciation
approachability
articulacy
assertiveness
assurance
attentiveness
attractiveness
audacity
availability
awareness
awe

b
balance
beauty
being the best

c
challenge
charity
charm
chastity
cheerfulness
clarity
cleanliness
clear-mindedness
cleverness
closeness
comfort
commitment
compassion
completion
composure
concentration
confidence
conformity
congruency
connection
craftiness
creativity
credibility
cunning
curiosity

d
daring
decisiveness
decorum
deference
delight
dependability
depth
desire
determination

devotion
devoutness
dexterity
dignity
diligence
direction

e
effectiveness
efficiency
elation
elegance
empathy
encouragement
endurance
energy
enjoyment
entertainment
enthusiasm
excellence
excitement
exhilaration
expectancy
expediency
experience
expertise
exploration
expressiveness

f
firmness
fitness
flexibility
flow
fluency
focus
fortitude

frankness
freedom
friendliness
frugality
fun

g
gallantry
gentility
giving
grace
gratitude
gregariousness
growth
guidance

h
happiness
harmony
health
heart
helpfulness
heroism
holiness
honesty
honor
hopefulness
hospitality
humility
humor
hygiene

i
imagination
impact
impartiality
independence
industry
ingenuity
inquisitiveness

insightfulness
inspiration
integrity
intelligence
intensity
intimacy
intrepidness
introversion
intuition
intuitiveness
inventiveness
investing

j
joy
judiciousness
justice

k
knowledge
kindness

l
leadership
learning
liberation
liberty
liveliness
logic
longevity
love

m
majesty
making a difference
mastery
maturity
meekness
mellowness
meticulousness

mindfulness
modesty
motivation
mysteriousness

n
neatness
nerve

o
obedience
open-mindedness
openness
optimism
order
organization
originality
outlandishness
outrageousness

p
passion
peace
perceptiveness
perfection
perkiness
perseverance
persistence
persuasiveness
piety
playfulness
pleasantness
pleasure
poise
polish
popularity
potency
power
practicality
pragmatism
precision

preparedness
presence
privacy
proactive
professionalism
prosperity
prudence
punctuality
purity

r
realism
reason
recognition
recreation
refinement
reflection
relaxation
reliability
religiousness
resilience
resolution
resolve
resourcefulness
respect
rest
restraint
reverence
richness

s
sacredness
sacrifice
sagacity
saintliness
sanguinity
satisfaction
security
self-control
selflessness

self-reliance
sensitivity
sensuality
serenity
service
sexuality
sharing
shrewdness
significance
silence
silliness
simplicity
sincerity
skillfulness
solidarity
solitude
soundness
speed
spirit
spirituality
spontaneity
spunk
stability
stealth
stillness
strength
Structure
Success
Supremacy
sympathy

t
teamwork
temperance
thankfulness
thoroughness
thoughtfulness
thrift
tidiness
timeliness

traditionalism
tranquility
transcendence
trust
trustworthiness
truth

u
understanding
unflappability
uniqueness
unity
usefulness
utility

v
valor
variety
victory
vigor
virtue
vision
vitality
vivacity

w
warmth
watchfulness
wealth
willfulness
willingness
winning
wisdom
wittiness
wonder

y
youthfulness

z
zeal

Self-value Mantra

*I am worthy to be truthful with myself
so that I can be authentic in my life.
I value myself enough to be real.
The values I live by are my reality
and not what I am told to value.
I live by my values because
they support positive actions in my life
and give me strength
to obtain realness in my everyday walk.*

Chapter Three
are you congruent with your beliefs?

I Believe

Your core beliefs are connected to your value system in that your beliefs are your outlook in how you view your world emotionally. Your beliefs paint the picture on your canvas that regulates your perception in life. The perception of who you are and what you believe can be of low vibration or high vibration, basically positive or negative. For example, do you believe that you are:

- Beautiful or ugly
- Smart or dumb
- Worthy or unworthy
- Positive or negative
- Shy or out going
- Lovable or unlovable
- Religious or spiritual
- Republican or democratic
- Tolerant or judgmental
- Dependable or undependable
- Success or failure
- Responsible or irresponsible
- Happy or sad

Here is an example of how core beliefs produce negative thoughts. Previously I described one of my adopted labels as "negative" and I rejected it. Before I rejected the label, I lived many years with the assumption that the label was true because for years, I thought I was not good enough to be smart.

This was one of my labels; 'Good thing you are cute, because you are not that smart.' For many years, I believed I was not smart and most definitely not worthy to go to college. This label painted my "not smart and not worthy" picture and produced these negative rules:

1. College is not for you, just stay home and be a loyal housewife.
2. If you voice your opinion, people will know you are dumb.
3. You will never get accepted into college because no one values your ideas.
4. Don't talk too much because people will see that you are just a hick from Arkansas.

In order for me to heal, I had to challenge all my beliefs from who I thought I was based on all these labels to what I really believed. I kept a journal to track and identify them because there were so many that some were not on a conscious level.

Not all of my beliefs were negative; some were positive. I made a list of all my moments of truth, positive and negative, and defined them. My moments of truth were significant moments that shifted my belief system because of my experience.

Here are some examples of both positive and negative beliefs:

1. I sang a song for my mom and she told me I had a beautiful voice. From that moment, I loved to sing and sang in the choir and performed solos.
2. I was riding my neighbor's pony and it ran me into a tree. From that moment on, I have been afraid of all horses because they are dangerous.
3. I was told I was not smart therefore I believed that I was not good enough.

In my moments of truth, I had to decide if they were empowering or disempowering to my life and health. For so many years I had held on to the disempowering moments of truth because of fear.

When I realized that horses were not dangerous and that I just needed a little experience in riding, I was not afraid of horses.

When I realized that I am smart and I am worthy, I went to college. Today I still sing and love it as a hobby and for spiritual therapy. My healing moments were realizing that I can let go of these disempowering moments of truth. When I realized they were disempowering, it was as easy as hitting the delete button.

Scan through your life and list all your moments of truth. After you list them, decide whether they are empowering or disempowering.

It is important to remember that you have the remote control to shift these beliefs. Ask yourself:

- *Why do I believe this?*
- *What is this belief costing me?*
- *What will happen if I let go of this belief?*

Changing your disempowering moments of truth is very simple: You just stop believing in them. Your only effort is to become aware enough to identify them.

An important key factor is that you must change your point of view in order to let go of your disempowering moment of truth. Disempowering beliefs attract negative responses.

Just deleting what is not good for you will help manifest new change.

I Believe Mantra

I believe that I can soar like an eagle
and that everything I believe in
is promoting high vibration.
I am a tower of creativity
and nothing can hold me back.
I rejoice in my beliefs
because they only manifest goodness
in my life and the life of others.

Chapter Four
attack your fear

Courage

For me, attacking my fear was the hardest step towards my healing process. It is one thing to have realized why I was sick and not happy, but to actually change my reality was one of the hardest tasks I have ever experienced.

I grew up with all the virtues of being a good woman to your man. It was something my mom and Mamah taught us girls at a very young age. We grew up with all the lessons in life to take care of our household, our children, and the man we marry. I was a good student because I was a good wife.

I had many boyfriends and loved and wanted to marry all of them. I just wanted to belong and have the perfect family. At the same time, one of my deep dark secrets was that I was attracted to some of the girls as well. When I was 13 years old, a neighbor, who was about 16, showed me her breasts. I shocked myself because I really enjoyed the look, however I felt guilty that I enjoyed it and truly believed it was wrong to feel that way. I also believed that if my parents knew how I felt, I would get into trouble.

I have an older cousin who is gay and I was really attracted to her life. I loved going to her house and spending the weekends with my Aunt just to watch my cousin and her girlfriend secretly exchange kisses behind my Aunt's back. My cousin was the only woman I knew at that time who was brave and independent. I was attracted to her personality and a little jealous of her free spirit. I felt that I was the opposite of being brave and independent. What I didn't like feeling was my perception that she was a rebel and that her actions might cause her to be alienated from her family. I could never be alienated because I needed my family to survive. I needed to belong so I kept my little secret and continued to strive to be the perfect person for everyone's needs. Besides, I knew I liked boys, and just thought I would grow out of my curious sinful interest in women.

At that point my only focus was to grow up and find the perfect man just like my mom did. I daydreamed of the wonderful life that I would have when I found the man of my dreams. I really believed in my perfect fairy tale and I knew it was only time that kept me from my husband and my family.

When I was 21, I married my husband who already had it all together. He had a college degree and owned his own business. He was quite the charmer and I could sit with him for hours listening to him tell stories. I loved that he had a ton of friends and that he was very well liked by everyone. Even though I missed being around my family, being around my husband gave me a whole new sense of belonging in that I had a new family.

Soon after moving into our first apartment I instantly began my wifely duties with ease. I had the entire apartment decorated perfectly and made sure he had a wonderful home to come home to at the end of the day. My entire life revolved around his needs, wants and desires. I did not complain as I had prepared for this my entire life.

At 24 I convinced him that we needed a baby. He was always busy with his life and I was getting bored just being a housewife. College was not an option because I always thought my role in life was to be a good mom and wife, and besides, I still thought I was not smart enough for college; therefore I felt I did not need the education. He did not want any children but I convinced him into believing that we would not conceive unless it was God's will. Still to this day, I can't believe that logic worked.

When our daughter was born, I had a whole new purpose in life. She became my heart and passion. I believe it was the first time I experienced what real love was. I had everything I wanted in life and nothing else could have been more perfect.

It was easy to take care of my husband. He was always doing something with his work or friends. I would leave him supper on the stove if he was going to be late and occasionally have sex with him when he wanted. Being his wife was a breeze. I took care of his needs and he made sure I had everything I needed materialistically. I loved being a mom. My daughter and I spent every moment together. I loved being her provider, protector and mom.

As our daughter got older and more independent I became bored again. I felt I needed more purpose, and for the first time in my life I thought about taking a few classes at the local community college. My husband was actually the one that encouraged me to do so as long as it didn't interfere with taking care of our daughter. He made it clear that she was my first priority, as his schedule was too busy, to be able to pick up any slack. So, I agreed and off to college I went.

I took all the classes that seemed fun to me at first, like Voice and Children's Literature. But the two classes that changed my life were Religion and Intrapersonal Relationships. I will get more into why my Religion class was so profound in a later chapter.

Most of the people in my Intrapersonal Relationships class were right out of high school, and a few students were older than me. I was 28 at the time. If I ever met an angel in real life it would have been my Intrapersonal Relationships professor. She was so loving and kind. I felt that when I was around her I was secure, like a warm blanket. I felt safe and I knew when I first met her, I could trust her.

After a couple of weeks in class, our assignment was to read the book, *"I'm OK-You're OK"* by Thomas A Harris, MD. As I started reading it, I realized that I am not the only one that felt I was not OK. I recall my professor saying "if we allow change in our life, we will still be OK". At that moment, tears started flowing and I was so embarrassed because I could not stop the emotion. It was as if she turned on the faucet and I did not know where the off switch was.

That class was a pivotal point in my life and I knew that I was on a new journey that would completely change my life, yet I had no clues as to what it was.

As I continued with my education, I became stronger and more independent, and my marriage was falling apart. I had already decided that when my daughter graduated from high school, I would probably get a divorce and get curious in my quest to find the true me. I had also decided that just being a good wife was not good enough, and by this time I felt my husband and I had already grown apart. We both lived separate lives even though we lived under the same roof.

My 4th year of college is when my dark ages began. I will not tell you the gossip of my life other than I came across the wrong man at the wrong time in my life. My search for happiness led me to the darkest place in my soul. When I did not find happiness in that journey, I humbly went back to my husband and he forgave me. I masked all my feelings and continued to be a good wife.

At this time I started getting sick and depressed and the doctors didn't help. I started seeking alternative therapy and, through the course of my healing, I was challenged to:

1. ***Review my identity***
2. ***Review my spiritual beliefs***
3. ***Review my nutritional intake***

I will talk about my spiritual beliefs and nutritional intake in a later chapter. When I started reviewing who I really was, it scared the hell out of me.

I met a woman who I adored and we became best friends. She was a massage therapist and very independent. She lived on her own and she was very intriguing to me. We spent hours talking on the phone and we spent as much time as we could together. She was the first friend that I felt the need to be completely transparent with. I knew I had to tell her about my bi-curious thoughts. I felt if I didn't tell her my deepest secrets, and somehow she found out, she would not remain my friend. When I did tell her, it did not change the fact that we were still best friends. She was the first friend that knew my deepest desires. Our friendship allowed me to gain the courage to grow the seed that was planted in my early college days.

A few years later, I met another woman who, after two years of friendship, I started having a crush on. She was not the first adult crush I had with a woman, but she was the first one I really was curious about. I could not get enough of her and could not understand why. I had never felt this compassionate about any of my friends in the past. She was different than any girlfriend I ever had and she was a lesbian.

I remember having a drink with her and we looked at each other in a way we had never done before. It was awkward but not enough to be embarrassing. Before I knew it, we engaged in a simple kiss on the lips. It was very short and sweet, yet at the same time, the most powerful kiss I had ever experienced. At that moment everything I had struggled with as far as my values and beliefs all made since. That simple kiss sent emotions and passion to the deepest part of my soul. I had never felt those feelings before; ever. I knew at that moment why I could never find happiness in me. I knew I had found my soul mate, she became my best friend.

She made it very clear to me that even though we kissed, she was not in a place where she could pursue a relationship with me and that any decision I made from here on could not include her. The only thing she could offer me was to continue to be my best friend. Wow, what the hell do I do now?

The next few days were painful. I had to finally deal with every emotion, every feeling, and every belief I had ever had.

- If I live this lifestyle, I will lose my family
- If I live this lifestyle, I will go to hell
- If I leave my husband, I will not have security
- If I leave my husband, I will lose friends
- If I leave my husband, I will have to be responsible financially
- If I leave my husband, I will lose my daughter

I cannot begin to describe the pain in my stomach or the grief and guilt in my heart. This was the first decision in my life that was about taking care of me, and not about taking care of someone else's needs. I had never been so afraid in all my life.

Despite my fear, I knew I had come to a point in my personal development where there was no return. I believed in myself and loved myself enough to attack my fears and move forward with my life.

Within four months of the decision to move forward in MY life, I moved out of my house, out of my 18 year marriage and was single. My condo was the first space that I really called my own. Even though I had been working on mental and spiritual healing, a part of my physical healing had just begun. For the first time in my life, I was dependant on me and not someone else. It was my first real home!

For the next three years my fears came true:

- I lost some of my friends
- I put a huge gap between me and my family
- My daughter blamed me for ruining her life
- I lost my relationship with the only God I knew
- I lost a man I truly loved as a friend

The only thing I had was my self-respect and my relationship with my new best friend, the woman I loved. Now, the only thing I could do was live for me and hope that those who I thought loved me would be part of my life again. If not, I had come to terms with the fact that it did not matter. The only important thing was loving myself enough to allow me to have soul freedom.

When I made that choice for me, everything started to fall into place. My relationship with the woman I loved became more than just friends. My daughter and I grew closer than ever before. My Mom accepted my life choices before she passed away, and my Step Dad loves me unconditionally just like he always had. My siblings still tease me but who cares.

Conquering my fears gave me the courage I needed to live my life for me. I knew that I was important and my feelings mattered. For the first time in my life I felt comfortable in my skin.

Please let me remind you that this chapter is NOT about coming out and being gay. It is about attacking your fears when you have reached a pivotal point in your life. It is about taking soulful steps in redefining your values and beliefs so that you are in balance with your Universe. Your pivot point may be a career change, divorce or other life shift. You may have lost a loved one or are considering moving to another town, state or country. You may be unsatisfied with your spiritual beliefs so whatever your pivot point is, be truthful with yourself. Stop living a lie for the sake of others or because of your own fears.

Courage Mantra

I will move forward no matter how afraid I am.
I have put on my armor of courage
and I will fear not
because I am worthy of my need to be free.
I am worthy to live my life comfortable in my skin.
Courage is my stepping stone
to my peace and joy.

Chapter Five
changing your rules

My Rules

We go through our entire life with rules. It starts as early as your mom's first "NO" while adapting to the family rules. Many go through their entire adult life not even questioning the validity of the rules they live by. Some rules we are aware of and others have been so deeply embedded, we are not even aware they exist. When we look at the value of these beliefs we go through the process of adaptation, and we accept its validity regardless of its benefits in our life.

As we go through life's journey we have shifts in our values and beliefs, and if we don't change the rules along the way we will find incongruent patterns that are not fitting with our new beliefs and values. The rules we live by can either:

1. Manifest positive outcome
2. Hold us back from what we really want
3. Keep us in denial of our true self

Rules should pave the way for what you want to manifest in life. They should never hold you back from obtaining the desires of your pure heart. Rules should always be challenged and tested.

As a young adult I lived by five rules:

1. Always take care of your husband no matter what. Divorce is not an option.
2. Be a good Born Again Christian and go to church every time the doors are open and tell everyone about Jesus.
3. Be everything to everyone so that you will be liked.
4. Be a better mom than mom was to me (even though mom was amazing).
5. Always have your house in order just in case someone stops by.

Most of these rules came from my environment such as family and church. Generally they are not bad/negative rules. Growing up, I took in all the rules from other people and made them my own. I even made important decisions about my life because of these rules, even though some were disempowering for me.

For years I lived by these rules despite the fact they were making me sick because I truly was not congruent. These rules fit my beliefs and values of my early years, but when those beliefs and values changed I did not change my rules, which left a huge disconnect.

Through the years (not actually knowing I did this) I took each rule and dissected it. This is the formula I used.

1. Where did the rule come from?
2. Do I still believe the rule to be true?
3. Is this rule serving me for my greater good?
4. Are these rules helping me obtain my wants, needs and desires?
5. How do my rules make me feel?

My revised rules:

1. I come first because I know when I am happy, my family and friends will be happy.
2. My spiritual journey is a personal experience and my mission is not to save souls but to make my life holy and sacred for my personal benefit and my relationship with the Divine.
3. Be everything to me so that I can have and attract healthy relationships that are meaningful and truly wanted.
4. Continue striving to be the best mom and meema. They deserve only the best of love and life.
5. I still believe my house should be in order but if it isn't, I try not to stress.

Personal Rules are good as long as you are clear they are serving your greater purpose. When they are congruent with your values and beliefs they serve to protect and guide you to your goals.

My Rules Mantra

My personal rules are my stepping stones for success.
They help to obtain positive actions
in order for me to accomplish my wants,
needs and desires.
Living by my personal rules
will help me soar to my dream
and the desires of my heart.

Chapter Six
embracing your new spirituality

I Am Perfect

Before embracing my new Spirituality I needed to review all of my past beliefs about God, church and religion. Redefining what I truly believed was the most fearful journey in my life, because I had to step outside my comfort zone in order to find my real peace and spiritual freedom.

Growing up I went to church most Sundays. My mom took advantage of the church bus picking us kids up and returning us several hours later. If truth be known, that was her church time; solitude from her five kids. I don't ever remember complaining because it gave me something to do.

So every Sunday I got in my Sunday dress and waited for the church bus to pick me up. I loved the ride because the church director gave us a donut and we sang songs all the way to church. It was a small Baptist church and because of my age, I had to go to children's church for worship.

I loved the Bible lessons and the stories about Jesus, but most importantly I loved the music. I loved the piano playing as I felt the vibrations of each note run through my body. My least favorite was the altar call because of the fear I had. If I didn't go to the "altar" to repent, I would be considered a bad child, so I usually went to the "altar" and repented every Sunday.

One Sunday we were learning a new song and it was a fast song with a good beat. "The lord told Noah, to build him an ark- key- ark-key, build it out of gofer barky-barky children of the Lord…………so rise and shine and give God the glory, glory…….." I loved this song so much that I jumped up and started dancing and singing and I felt so proud to rejoice in praise. I was not even a minute into my dance and I looked up to see the deacon of children's church take my arm and escort me into the hall.

The deacon was a tall man with slicked back hair and smelt of tobacco and body odor topped with a nasty musk smell. I still had the song stuck in my head and the joy in my heart. I was clueless as to why he brought me to the hall. I remember looking up to him as he bent down and got in my face and said, " Young lady, we do not dance in church because it is a sin, and if you want forgiveness make sure you go to the altar and repent". During altar call, I remember him standing by my row where I was sitting, looking at me with meanness in his eyes, so I went to the "altar" and repented for dancing in church.

Out of this particular Baptist Church experience I adopted these rules:

1. It's a sin to dance in church.
2. If you do not accept Jesus in your heart you will go to hell.
3. Women are not allowed to become preachers.
4. If you repent you are forgiven.
5. You can't have sex before you are married.
6. You can never get a tattoo.
7. You can't be a drunk.
8. You can't be unfaithful to your spouse.
9. Your job is to win souls to Christ.
10. You can love no other God.
11. You can't be gay.
12. You can't murder anyone.
13. God is the judge and he is a jealous God.

When I lived in Texas, I had a break from Church. Mom never went and always told us it was not important for her to go because Jesus will always be in her heart and that her Holy Spirit will always guide her.

When we moved to Belgium I was introduced to God in a whole new way. As I mentioned before, my first boyfriend was from a group of missionaries that belonged to Assembly of God Church. They had the same rules but added a few more elements to the mix and dancing in church was not a sin. They told me that in order to go to heaven one should be born again. In order to be born again, I needed to be filled with the Holy Spirit. When you are filled with the Spirit you will have gifts that will help you in your Christian walk. Among these gifts were the gift of tongues and the gift of prophecy.

They also believed the Devil lurked around seeking to destroy, and if you entertained him, you could possibly be possessed or oppressed. They enforced all their rules with the fear of having a demonic oppression or possession. I was one of those people that went all in, all of the time. Looking back, mom and I fought the most when I became born again as it was my duty to constantly remind her that she is going to hell because she smokes and drinks and because she is not born again. I truly thought at one time my mom was possessed by the devil because she did not believe the way I did.

I carried all of these beliefs with me in my adult life not questioning them. These rules and beliefs were my spiritual foundation and it's really all I knew, and I was afraid to question them because I was truly afraid of going to Hell.

When I realized that my religious beliefs and my need to be with this woman were not congruent, I thought I had to choose between God and my authenticity. It did not happen overnight, but I abandoned God because I did not believe I could have both.

After a few years I remembered what my religion professor in college had said about one Divine, and that many roads lead to that Divine. It made me curious because I really missed communicating with God. I missed my prayer time and I missed having the power of belief in something bigger than me. I missed having God in my life.

I started talking and praying to God again but this time it was in my own way, without the influence of a church or pastor's interpretations of the bible. I wanted to know the truth about God without the help of another human being. The more I talked to God, the stronger I got. The more I listened to the Spirit in my heart, the more I received healing from all the dogma that held me like a prisoner. I also met a woman that took me back to my Shaman roots and showed me spirituality the way my ancestors believed. I started to become whole again and realized that I never had to leave God, because God is universal energy that manifests in everyone and everything. Once I realized that the God I abandoned was not real and that the real light of God was pure love and energy, I became what I call organically born again.

My relationship with God and my spiritual habits got stronger because I no longer walked in judgment or believed in rules that were not serving my higher purpose or the good of all mankind. For the first time in my life I felt God's true love in my heart. For the first time I knew that God never left me, and most importantly, God approves of who I am.

By opening my heart to the unconditional God of love, I have learned so many truths about life, energy and healing. I realized that my new beliefs were pure and that my gifts were meant to heal the world.

Looking back in my spiritual walk, I was saved and baptized, born again but never felt God's love greater than when I gave up:

- Judging others for their beliefs
- Living in fear
- Living in condemnation
- Believing "some way" is the only way
- Living incongruent to me

Giving up these beliefs allowed me to see true enlightenment. I found my own unique path to God. For the first time I truly felt I was organically born again.

I Am Perfect Mantra

I am worthy of unconditional love.
In me lives the spirit of the Divine
which manifests goodness and pure love.
I am a perfect creature in God's universe.
When I walk in this organic light,
there are no walls separating the Divine energy
yet many souls obtaining soulful freedom.

Chapter Seven
letting go of the old you

Soul Freedom

Most of us celebrate common rites of passage such as high school graduation, college or marriage, but we fail to recognize other significant life journeys along the way. All of our journeys that cause us to redefine who we are or how we relate to the world around us deserve to be recognized with a ritual or celebration. Recognizing the shifts in our life through a ceremony acknowledges the changes that have occurred and can reinforce our new beliefs, values and rules.

I wanted to create ceremonial blessings for my new identity, my new beliefs and my new body. I also wanted to clear from my personal space all the old stagnant energy and invoke new energies with new intentions that would create the space for me to grow and be inspired according to my wants, needs and desires.

I felt it important to create this celebration ceremony in honor of me. I hope you use this ceremony to create the same blessings for you. Feel free to personalize it in order to make it comfortable for you.

The steps are...

1. Sacred Space Ceremony
2. Soulful Freedom Ceremony

Sacred Space Ceremony

This blessing is one that will help you clear out negative energy and celebrate the creation of new energy in regards to the new belief system you have created.

As you work to create new spaces in your life, both physical and spiritual, use this blessing ceremony to celebrate and bring the energy to its fullest vibration.

If you do not want to use the ceremony I use you can create your own. I use these steps to create **Sacred Space**:

1. Prepare
2. Set Intensions
3. Purify
4. Invoke
5. Maintain

The Ceremony
Intention
Clear all negative energy and establish positive energy that will provide encouragement to live by your new belief system.

Materials:

- Small candle; matches
- Sage Smudge Stick
- Feather (optional)
- Small ceramic bowl of spring water lavender flowers or essential oil

Make sure before you begin, you are alone and there are no interruptions.

1. On your kitchen table, place all your materials needed for this ceremony.

2. Take a deep breath and Light the candle with your intentions.

3. Light your smudge stick and walk around your house fanning the smoke with the intention of clearing the space to fully invoke the energy of your intention. Do this as long as you feel you need to, keeping your awareness focused on the positive and productive energy that is intended for your home. After you have completed this, take your smudge stick back to the kitchen table and allow it to continue burning (in a fireproof dish).

4. Go back to each room and stand in the center of the room. Close your eyes and deeply feel the vibrations of the space, the energy you have created within it, and the effects you intend. Say the blessing below or one that you have written that is specific to the space:

   Bless this space. Allow the feelings and thoughts of my new belief system to come alive, to live in high vibration and to experience love unconditionally in this home. Bless this space.

5. Go back to the kitchen and complete the blessing by dipping your finger tips into the small bowl of lavender water and sprinkling it around the space in each room. After you sprinkle each corner or area of the room, make the infinity sign (a sideways figure eight) with your hand to seal the intention of your ceremony. As you do this, continue to bless the space by invoking blessings.

6. Go back to the kitchen where you started and spend some time reflecting upon your ceremony and the wonderful accomplishments you have made in this celebration. Allow yourself to experience the full realization of its potential. After you feel you are ready to celebrate the new energy, complete the blessing by blowing out the candle while saying, I have soulful freedom.

7. Place the box from your Soulful Freedom Ceremony© somewhere in your kitchen as a reminder of your new transformation.

8. Make sure you express gratitude when you are finished with your ceremony.

9. Place a bouquet of flowers as offering to seal the energy in the space you have blessed on your kitchen table.

Soulful Freedom Ceremony©

Make sure you pick a space to perform your ceremony that is positive energy with zero interruptions so that your end result will be sacred and meaningful.

Intent

Strength, Power, Courage and Individuality

Materials:

- 20 white pillar/votive candles for inner strength
- Pillow to sit upon on the floor/ground
- Dark Red fabric which represents courage and movement towards individuation by crossing the path of one circle to the other
- A smaller piece of fabric used for table cloth or a small altar table
- Bowl of spring water
- Pen and Journal
- A copy of your new values, beliefs and rules
- A list of virtues
- 2 new votive or column candles—red (root of life) and white (spiritual purity)
- Small crystal quartz
- Small box
- A selection of music (optional)

Ceremonial Flow

1. Make two separate circles with the 20 candles, big enough for you to sit in them (the circles need to be close together). Create a sacred space by placing the materials on a piece of fabric/tablecloth. The pillow and the tablecloth with materials are placed in the middle of one of the circles of candles. Place the red fabric at the outer part of your 1st circle creating a pathway for you to enter the 2ndcircle. Place the red candle in the 2nd circle with matches.

2. Light the candles forming both circles and sit in the first circle on your pillow.

3. Light the white candle, focusing on the sanctity of the celebration. Place your crystal in front of the candle. Summon the crystal to hold space of your intentions. Focus on the crystal as you read the blessing.

4. Say the following blessing:

   I begin this soulful freedom ceremony with the power of good intentions.

   As I accept the death of my old values, beliefs and rules, I honor the lessons I have learned and welcome opportunity to grow, to learn, and to build. I have the strength and courage to complete the tasks necessary for my new beliefs. Bless this ceremony as I move forward into action.

5. Pause and reflect upon your list of new values, beliefs and rules. Consider the actions that you took that allowed yourself to get to this point.

6. These are actions that you accomplished in honor of you. Take a moment to allow yourself to feel the strength it took for you to get to this beautiful place in your life.

7. Take your list of virtues and circle as many virtues that are important to your values.

8. Place the crystal stone in the bowl of spring water as you are immersing your new values, beliefs, rules and virtues in the emotions of your new life. How does it feel knowing you have put yourself first and accomplished such sacred work?

9. Remove the crystal and place it in your box along with your list of values, beliefs, rules and virtues. Write in your journal ideas and inspirations along with some new goals that came to you during your ceremony.

10. Take the bowl of spring water and pour it out on the ground (or folded towel if you are inside) as the water leaves the bowl, use your mind to create the intention of how your new life will flow with ease.

11. Blow out the white candle and express gratitude for all your life's journeys.

12. Take your box and journal and walk across the dark red fabric that represents courage. As you are walking across, do not look back as you are leaving your old values, beliefs and rules behind. Allow yourself to feel that feeling.

13. As you step into your Soulful Freedom Circle© light your red candle that represents root grounding. Place your box with journal beside the candle and raise your arms in the air. Feel the power that is in the circle. Allow all of the power in that circle to come in to the bottom of your feet and fill your entire body with love, strength, courage, peace and wisdom. Take your hands and place them on your heart and say the following mantra out loud.

Soul Freedom Mantra

I am worthy of my life
and I give myself permission
to change my structure of beliefs.
I give myself passage to live in congruency
with my feelings, wants and needs rather than others.
I honor my new values, beliefs and rules.
I will live by the virtues
that are congruent with my feelings.
I will live everyday
in the power of love and in the moment of joy.

14. Blow out your candle and embrace becoming the new you, organically born again.

15. Put your box in the kitchen where it will always remind you to be mindful of your new life.

The Blessing is complete.

Now that you are finished with both of your ceremonies, allow yourself to celebrate your new life by doing one of the following or something of the same nature.

- Take a walk on the beach or lake
- Get a massage
- Get a manicure and pedicure
- Go zip lining
- Take a day trip
- Buy yourself a piece of jewelry to signify your new you
- Cook your favorite meal

Chapter Eight
learning to live in a sacred vibration

Positive Vibration

For years I struggled and made choices that were not serving my higher purpose. I lived by beliefs that were negative in my life. I walked in guilt, shame and fear because of someone else's influence and beliefs for my life. When I became mindful of my own actions and beliefs, positive shifts started manifesting. My vibrations were higher because I started manifesting more love and less guilt in my life.

Life is all about choices, and for every action there is a reaction. We choose how we live our life. Including how we feel. The power of our energy can either move mountains or cause death. If your energy is vibrating at a level that is not productive you may be vibrating at a TOXIC LEVEL which can hold you back from accomplishing goals and obtaining the desires of your heart.

How many people do you know who are struggling? Maybe they are having financial difficulties or personal conflicts in their life. No matter what happens they view life as a constant bumpy rollercoaster with negative events that continually hold them back.

No one is exempt from struggles, we all have them and we know that life is about the good days and the bad days. We all want to reach the desires of our hearts. We want to live life accomplishing our goals and being happy and healthy. So the answer to the question, "Why do we struggle?" depends on what level your energetic vibration is.

Quantum physics has determined that everything in the universe has energy. Your electromagnetic vibrations resonate at varying frequencies that align to your thoughts, feelings, beliefs and rules. One of the most common causes of low vibration energy is negative thought: telling yourself things like "I'm such a loser" or "My struggles are just the way it always is." When we allow our struggles to control our mindset, we devalue our beliefs and values. We live in a "suffer" mode, which is caused by a negative anchor. We start to focus all of our feelings on negative thoughts and begin to feel lesser, because we are comparing ourselves to those around us...who are also in "suffer" mode!

Sometimes we can't change our struggles, but we can change our mindset by learning to become transparent and letting go of all the beliefs, values and rules that are disempowering. Surprisingly, when we let go of those negative anchors our suffering diminishes. These beliefs are limiting because of the universal Law of Attraction, which basically states, 'you achieve what you believe'. This law also incorporates the principle that you attract what you focus on. If you think and feel worried about what you don't want, that is often what will occur.

Lower vibration in such emotions as fear, anger, depression, doubt, frustration and judgment sooner or later shut people down and can cause mental and physical exhaustion.

Going back to the Law of Attraction, it is important to make sure your place of worship is of higher vibration and not one that promotes judgment or condemnation. It is spiritually toxic to be made to feel shame, guilt or hate. Places of worship that offer these bullets are the healthiest choices.

- A structure for self discovery
- Promotes individual spiritual growth

When we start focusing on ourselves and only comparing our self to "our past self," we can then move forward in a progression that is healthy. We can bring value to our lives and to the world around us.

People with high vibration energy are optimistic, enthusiastic, passionate and happy; their magnetic energy draws other people to them. Usually they have such joy and love of life; they attract people, money and success easily and effortlessly.

When an individual begins to live in a higher energy vibration, it allows you to focus on the now and walk in a sacred light by becoming the new you; organically born again.

No one is perfect and we are going to have moments of low vibration, after all, we are human. If we make our self-accountable we can measure our emotions daily and make sure we are on constant mindfulness of living a higher vibration. I call this mindset my emotional delivery truck that transports emotions all day and is always carrying different types of emotional baggage.

My toxic baggage is when I am:

- Judging others
- Feeling shame
- Having a bitter heart
- When I am jealous
- When I hate someone because they are different
- Feeling lesser than
- Feeling unloved
- Feeling insecure
- Feeling not good enough
- Feeling invalidated
- Comparing myself to others

These are the toxic emotions that I want to get rid of as soon as one is loaded onto my emotional delivery truck. As soon as it loads, I feel the weight and realize it's overload. These are feelings you do not want to harbor or entertain; it is important to get rid of them as fast as you can. They do not serve any purpose in your life.

My fragile baggage is when I am:

- Being transparent
- Defining my beliefs and values
- Redefining my rules
- Setting goals
- Personalizing my spiritual life
- Letting go of negative anchors
- Trying to be congruent with my feelings

This baggage is fragile because you are in transformation mode. You are dealing with some of your toxic emotions that may hold you back from delivering this fragile baggage in your life. These are emotions to get curious with. Challenge yourself to become the best you can be for you.

My precious cargo baggage is when I am:

- Living in unconditional love
- Living in balance
- Feeling confident
- Developing positive Spiritual habits
- Meditating and communicating with the Divine
- Allowing myself to feel joy
- Having peace
- Living in the moment
- Experiencing Soulful Freedom©

This cargo is most sacred. It is a load that takes time to deliver. It requires a daily check on transparency. If you are diligent and master these spiritual points, you will be living in your highest vibration.

If we set standards in our life and in our hearts, we can accomplish anything. If we want to be happy, we can just turn on the switch. If we want to feel joy, we just give ourselves permission. By learning to live in the moment and allowing yourself to go through the healing process of making sure we are congruent with our beliefs and values we will experience Soulful Freedom©. I know, because I did. I know, because I still do.

Positive Vibration Mantra

*I free my mind, body and soul
from toxic thoughts that drag me down.
I stand firm in my ability to be mindful
in living every moment
with positive vibrations
that support my spiritual growth.
I am a temple and only goodness grows in my soul.*

Chapter Nine
becoming spiritually empowered

In the Light

I think the biggest mistake people make in their spiritual walk is that they believe being involved in a religious organization automatically makes one close to God when in fact, this is not true. Being close to God means YOU spend solitude and communicate with YOUR Divine.

For many years I worshiped a God that did not even love who I was, and in order for me to be one with that God, I had to not be me. I lived a devoted life, going to church and doing what I was told. It was only when I started getting curious to test its validity for my life, that I found my soul's freedom.

Having a relationship with YOUR Divine is like hanging out with your best friend. The more you are together, the closer you are. The more you communicate, the better you understand one another. The more you communicate and seek your divine, the more spiritual you will become. When you seek out your own relationship with God, without the influence of another, you will experience what it means to be organically born again.

A few of the tools to enhance my relationship with God are:
- Mantras
- Prayers
- Meditation
- Writing in your Spiritual journal
- Striving to live in a higher vibration (Chapter 8)
- Implementing virtues (Chapter 13)

Mantras

The dictionary describes a Mantra as a sacred utterance (syllable, word, or verse) believed to possess mystical or spiritual power.

Mantras may be spoken aloud or uttered in thought, and they may be either repeated or sounded only once. Most have no apparent verbal meaning, but they are thought to have profound significance and serve as distillations of spiritual wisdom.

Repetition of a mantra can induce a trance-like state and can lead the participant to a higher level of Spiritual awareness.

My definition of a Mantra is a sound, **or writing,** that ignites transformation.

For thousands of years, some of the most enlightened Spiritual leaders have been using Mantras/affirmations for spiritual growth. Mantras are powerful tools to help empower spirituality and help create the life you desire. They help you get into higher vibrations of clarity and focus. When practiced, one becomes enriched with purpose, love and peace.

There are five steps in creating your personal Mantra:

Step One
Make sure your Mantra is positive. Use only words that support the higher vibration feelings such as confidence, self-love, strength and courage. Avoid words that support the lower vibration feelings such as shame, guilt, hate or self-doubt.

Step Two
What is your intention? You can create a Mantra for the purpose of spiritual enhancement, personal development, career goals, health, family, etc. Be clear on what you want, need and desire when writing and practicing your Mantra. Before you actually write your mantra, write down what you want to accomplish. By doing this you will be more effective with writing more authentic words to be used in your Mantra.

Step Three
Write your Mantra. Write a sentence or phrase that attracts what you want. Here are a few examples:
- Each day I become a stronger person.
- I love foods that are healthy for my body.
- I feel balanced and centered in my life.
- I am creative and able.
- Money comes to me effortlessly and with ease.
- I am a money magnet.
- I am worthy of God's love.
- I love connecting to my higher self.
- I love and am loved unconditionally.
- I have amazing friends that support and uplift me.
- I am a beautiful human being.
- I accept myself completely, here and now.
- I have everything I need and I am perfect.
- I am exactly where I am supposed to be.

Remember, you can write more than a sentence but make sure they are not too long so that they are easier to remember. Once you write your Mantra, say it out loud and make sure it resonates with you. Does your Mantra feel empowering?

Step Four
It is not only important to say the Mantra, but it is also just as important to feel your Mantra and integrate that feeling in your entire body. You need to say it, you need to believe it, and you need to feel it so that it becomes your reality.

Saying + Believing + Feeling = Manifesting Reality

Step Five
When you write your Mantra, don't put it away for safe keeping. Practice saying it. Repeat your Mantra daily and memorize it. Place it on your bathroom mirror or a place where you will see it daily. Remember that it takes discipline to create consistency, and when you are consistent you will enhance your spiritual habits.

To review and be an expert on writing your own Mantras remember to:
- Be positive
- Have intention
- Write your Mantras
- Feel them in your body
- Practice

In addition to writing my own Mantras I also enjoy practicing Bija Mantras. (B AH - h ah, meaning seed) Bija Mantras are one syllable Mantras that activate your chakras, which are your energy centers. When your chakras are fully open, your energy flows in balance with your Universe.

The seven cleansing Bija Mantras that activate chakras are:
- "LAM"- root chakra (Said like lum as in alum)
- "VAM"- sacral chakra (vum as in thumb)
- "RAM"- core chakra (rum)
- "YAM"- heart chakra (yum as in yummy)
- "HAM"- throat chakra HAM (hum/ humming)
- "OM"- third eye chakra (u as in uber)
- "OM"- crown chakra (aum)

Chant the Bija Mantras, either one at a time or in sequences. Repetition can help you access a meditative state.

Prayers

The dictionary defines prayer as a silent or spoken petition made to God or a god. Prayer has been practiced in all religions throughout history. Its characteristic postures (bowing the head, kneeling, prostration) and position of the hands (raised, outstretched, clasped) signify an attitude of submission and devotion.

My definition of prayer is developing a beautiful relationship through daily/sacred conversations with your Divine.

Learning to pray is as simple as communicating with your best friend. There is no right way or wrong way to pray, however there are different types of prayers and one should be aware and mindful which type of prayer is needed when praying.

There are prayers of:
- Praise
- Request
- Seeking
- Gratitude
- Interceding

Although there are more types of prayers, these are the ones we will focus on to obtain soulful freedom.

Before you start praying you should decide what to call your Divine. Remember that whatever name you choose is the right name for you. God does not care about the name as much as the relationship you are building.

The names I personally use are...
- Father God
- Goddess of the Universe
- Mother Earth
- Great Spirit
- Divine Master

The format that I use is just like writing a letter
1. Dear _____
2. Start with gratitude
3. Body of prayer

When we praise God through prayer, we are expressing favor and glorifying perfection in God.
- I praise you for your perfect timing.
- I praise you for your unconditional love.
- I praise you for the beautiful earth I call home.

When we request through prayer, we are asking for something in our life.
- Give me hope.
- Give me strength.
- Give me courage.

When we seek through prayer we are searching for answers in our life.
- Help me to understand.
- Give me wisdom.
- Help me to learn the truth.

When we offer prayers of gratitude we are expressing thankfulness of the miracles in our life. We are in the state of being grateful.
- I am grateful for my life.
- I am grateful for my freedom.
- I am grateful for my ability to love myself.

When we offer interceding prayers we are praying for someone else. This is more advanced spiritual work because your petition has to be without judgment.
- I pray for his/her healing.
- I pray for his/her protection.
- I pray for his/her safety.

It is important not to pray for someone because you judge them.
- I pray for his/her salvation.
- I pray for him/her to be a better person.
- I pray for his/her lack of knowledge.

These prayers are self-centered and judgmental. They will not even get to the Divine because of their low vibration energy.

Meditation

The dictionary defines meditation as a private religious devotion or mental exercise, in which techniques of concentration and contemplation are used to reach a heightened level of spiritual awareness. The practice has existed in all religions since ancient times.

My definition of mediation is learning to breathe so that I can reach a place of solitude to hear the voices of my Divine spirits. In my opinion, if you do not include meditation with prayer you are having a one-sided conversation.

Prayer + Meditation = Relationship with God

It is important to allow yourself solitude when meditating. Distractions will only frustrate you and dishonor what you are trying to accomplish. You need to find a quiet place. If you don't have one at home, go to the park or a parking lot, somewhere that is safe, a place of solitude. Create time everyday for your meditation and be faithful. Remember, the more you practice, the better you will get.

Before you start to meditate, set your intention. Maybe you want answers from your Divine. Maybe you want to focus on personal or business matters. Maybe you just need to relax. By setting your intention you will be more focused and open to allow a natural flow of energy throughout your body.

Once you allow yourself to feel your body, let everything else relax, and soften. Breathing through the nose, loosen the face, neck, hands, and stomach area. You may want to begin at the head and move your attention slowly downward, methodically relaxing and softening each part of the body. Allow your body to relax and just let go! Consciously releasing body tension will help you be open to whatever comes up during your meditation.

While breathing is a function most people take for granted, rarely is it practiced correctly. Before learning to meditate it is essential that you learn how to breathe properly and fully:

- Lie down on a rug, or blanket, on the floor with your legs relaxed and slightly apart, your toes lying comfortably outwards, arms at your sides not touching your body, your palms up, and your eyes closed. This is called a "relaxed body" position. Take time to relax your body and breathe freely.

- It is best to breathe through your nose. Keep your mouth closed as you breathe.

- As you breathe, your chest and abdomen should move together. If only the chest seems to rise and fall, your breathing is shallow and you are not making good use of the lower part of your lungs.

As you inhale you should feel your abdomen rising; it is as if your stomach is filling with air. As you exhale, the abdomen comes back in, like a balloon releasing all of its air. This inhale and exhale process should continue comfortably and smoothly.

- When you inhale count 1,2,3,4,5,6 and when you exhale count 1,2,3,4,5,6,7,8 making sure your counts are the same one second timing.

When you learn to breathe you will be able to put your body into a deep state of relaxation. Your body will relax to the point that your body aches will diminish.

Choose an object to concentrate on during your meditation. If you are outside use a tree or flower. If you are inside use a candle. Whatever object you select, stay with it for at least seven to 10 breaths. If your mind wanders gently lead your attention back to the chosen object of meditation. Your intention and consistency are the key factors for creating awareness, not the number of times your mind wanders.

When you have reached those moments of solitude, when you are just focusing on your breath and your intention, this is when you can "hear" the voice of your Divine. Remember "hearing" may not be literal. You may get a feeling, a sensation or just a knowing. Allow yourself to "hear" what your body is feeling.

It is important to remember that the more you practice, the faster you will learn to master the qualities of concentration and mindfulness. Concentration is the ability to put your attention into one place, your intention. Mindfulness is simply being aware. Without concentration and mindfulness, meditation is difficult to carry out.

Here are some tips to remember:
- Sit still every day, even if it's for a short period.
- Practice breathing every night at bedtime.
- The more you practice, the better you get.
- Relax and do not stress.

- Try to give yourself solitude daily.
- Treat meditation as something sacred and not as a chore.
- If you miss a day, a week, or a month — simply begin again.
- If you need guidance, ask for help from an experienced practitioner.

Writing in Your Spiritual Journal

We remember a very small percentage of what happens to us each day. We also forget most of our feelings and reactions to what happens to us. If we write these feelings down in a journal, we have the ability to see connections that give us complete clarity.

A spiritual journal is a great way to track how you are growing spiritually. Spiritual journals focus on your spiritual self, your growth, your spiritual experiences and the Divine wisdom that is given to you through your spiritual practice. Keeping a spiritual journal can aid you in becoming spiritually empowered.

Invest in a nice journal and make sure it is just for spiritual purposes only. This is your sacred tool for collecting all your knowledge and experiences. It should be kept in a private place and respected as holy in your spiritual journey.

During your spiritual break, allow yourself to reflect on your spiritual journey. You may look at how you are feeling and examine why you feel that way. Here is a list of things you can include in your spiritual journal:
- Insights from your spiritual break/daily life.
- Specific prayers you have prayed.
- God's answers to your prayers.
- Spiritual needs.
- Meaningful quotations.
- Lessons you have learned.
- Daily events of personal or spiritual significance.
- Praise and gratitude.
- Things you sensed around you (observations).
- Places you've been and spiritual connections you've drawn from them.
- Things you've discovered while looking back in the journal.

Here is a list of questions you might want to answer in your journal. These questions will help you go deeper in your spiritual awareness so that you can strive towards your own Soulful Freedom®.

1. How would you describe your spiritual journey over the years? What has changed for you and/or remained the same.

2. What is your own sense of your spirituality now? Briefly describe your spirituality, your experiences, beliefs and values.

3. What is the significance for your spiritual journey right now? What can you learn from this and how might you live your life to increase your awareness of something greater?

4. How do you nurture your soul? What do you do that gives you a sense of fullness in your life?

5. What is missing from your spiritual development? What do you hunger for? What do you still seek?

6. Does your belief system encourage reasoning and questioning or does your system require you to accept beliefs you can't challenge?

7. Why have you chosen your belief system over others? If you consider it the best choice, how did you reach your conclusion?

8. Would you change your belief system in any way if you could? If yes, what would that change be and what stops you from making that change?

Remember, there's no wrong way to keep a journal, just as there's no wrong way to pray. If it works for you, it's right. Becoming spiritually empowered and experiencing Soulful Freedom® is a personal experience that only you can walk. It is yours and yours alone.

In the Light Mantra

Great Spirit,
You are beautiful and I crave to seek your face,
feel the power of your earth
and your Divine presence in my heart.
I see your grace when I walk the earth.
I feel your love when I open my heart.
I experience your power when I believe.
For in you, I have found my Soulful Freedom.

Chapter Ten
taking care of your temple

Self-honor

Taking care of your temple is to live your life organically. Eat healthy, practice positive living and make it a habit to live life in the moment in your Soulful Freedom®.

The definition of health is the condition of the mind or body in reference to soundness and vigor; freedom from disease or ailment. When taking care of your temple I believe that your Spirit should also be free from disease or ailment. So the principals of this chapter address health as a condition by which your mind, body and soul live vigorously free from dis-ease!

Health is a physical, mental, emotional and spiritual force in the universe, it is energy. In fact, the body is an energy system. Organs are simply trillions of cells with vibration patterns all working together to make you who you are. We also have life force energy we call "chi," and there are emotions associated with all the organs and structures of your body. Ancient healers have been measuring energy and vibrations for centuries and understand the balance in lifestyle. Health is making sure your energy and vibrations are of honor and respect to your body. When you take responsibility for your energy, you understand health is energy.

To be healthy, our energy needs to be balanced. The food we eat needs to nourish our body and our attitudes need to nourish our spirit. So in looking at health and what constitutes the best food for us to eat, we need to look at exactly what it is that causes our cells not only to survive, but more importantly, to thrive. In addition, it is important to look at how our attitudes affect our performance and the lives of others around us. To find the ultimate recipe for health we need to be aware what our body, mind, and soul need to thrive.

The recipe for taking care of your temple:
1. Detoxify your body
2. Purify your negative emotions
3. Nourish your body with healthy foods

In other words, to maximize our health, we need to make better food choices, learn to get rid of toxic emotions and learn to eat healthy.

Food is our most potent medicine. Clinical studies have proven that proper nutrition plays a significant role in dis-ease prevention and the restoration of health. Whole food nutrition allows the body to use its built-in healing ability, and will assist the body's capacity to heal itself.

I believe that awareness and education are the first steps in addressing our health problems. Improving how we eat and our lifestyle habits is one of the most critical things we can do in improving the quality of our life immediately and into the future as we age.

Step One
Detoxification
Detoxification is a normal process within the body, as it neutralizes and eliminates toxins through the major organs such as our colon, liver, kidneys, lungs, lymph and skin.

Food additives are substances that are not natural in the foods we eat. Additives are for the purpose of coloring and preserving. The FDA lists thousands of chemicals that are deliberately added into our food supply, many of which are not legal for use in other countries.

The bottom line is additives are used to make as much money as possible in as little time as possible. Those involved in food production use whatever methods they can, within legal limits, to increase their bottom line. These methods include:

- Using hormones and antibiotics to shorten the length of time needed to fatten the animal to market weight.
- Using preservatives to extend the shelf life of food.
- Coloring oranges, waxing apples, and bleaching flour for consumer eye appeal.
- Using pesticides on produce.
- Using cheaper ingredients, or synthetic rather than natural ingredients, to decrease product cost.
- Using artificial sweeteners and imitation oils to meet consumer demand for low calorie products.

Chronic exposure to additives occurs when a person consumes chemicals in small quantities over a long period of time. The effects are cumulative and tend to worsen over time. Gallbladder problems are a major factor in chemical toxicity. Over 35% of the population has had their gallbladder removed, making this one of the most common surgeries. Other conditions such as memory loss, personality changes, dizziness, vision problems, liver and kidney damage, skin irritation, fatigue and depression can be attributed to exposure of chemicals consumed in foods.

Unfortunately, we have been conditioned to want picture-perfect produce and processed non-foods. The end result is that the marketplace is full of unnatural chemicals and foods which can do the body more harm than good. If you don't believe me, let me give you a visual. Imagine seeing a swimming pool your age that has never been cleaned. What would that pool look like? My visual is muck and chemical mush slouching around in your body while millions of parasites are swimming around looking for food. If you are not aware of what you are eating, your internal organs may very well look like the mucky water of a dirty swimming pool.

Here is a checklist to see if you are in need of a detox program.
- Do you feel bloated, constipated?
- Do you feel tired and have low energy?
- Do you eat processed foods?
- Are your hair and skin not looking as healthy as they used to?
- Do you eat junk food more than once per week?
- Do you frequently get infections and colds?
- Do you feel you need to clear out the cobwebs in your brain?

If you have answered yes to three or more of the above questions then a detoxification might be just what your body needs to regain balance.

Before you detoxify on any program, ask your doctor if it is safe for you!

Although 10 to 21 days allows the most time for your body to really begin the detoxification process properly, I've found that most people can only manage up to three days if they have a busy lifestyle. If you can do seven days that's great, if you can do 10 days that's even better, if you can only do one day, then that is better than none. However, I recommend that if you can at least commit to three days, you will begin to see the real value in detoxification.

So what are the benefits?
- You eliminate stored waste, and for some that means they will lose weight
- Improved vitality and energy levels right away
- Improved circulation through purifying the liver and blood
- Enhanced mental clarity
- Cravings will diminish
- Your body will be closer to a sacred vibration.

There are many different detoxification products and programs, and I believe that a program that is not too extreme and one that does not leave you starving is one which is most achievable and easiest to commit to. For best results, do not substitute any ingredients in this program.

At the end of the day this program will make you feel and look amazing!

The Program
On Rising
Drink an 8 ounce glass of detoxification water.

Detoxification Water Recipe
- 2 lemons, sliced
- 1 cucumber, sliced
- 12 mint leaves
- 2 liters of spring water

Set overnight. Always keep a pitcher of detoxification water in your refrigerator. It is a healthy way to start your day.

Before Breakfast
Drink 16 ounces of Hunter Wellness Mojo juice.
Ingredients:
- 3 big leaves of kale (stem and all)
- 2 handfuls of spinach
- 1 handful of Spring Mix Greens
- 1 kiwi fruit (sliced but not peeled)
- 6 grapes
- 6 Mint leaves
- Slice of fresh peeled ginger
- 2 ounces of water (ice cold)
- 8 cubes of ice

Blend in your blender, Vita Mix or food processor
I personally find that my Vita Mix works the best.

Breakfast
Eat any fresh fruits, along with any combination of lettuce, celery, and avocado, if desired. Be sure to have avocado with fruit as the fatty acids will help satisfy you until your next meal.

Do not blend your breakfast into a smoothie.

Between Breakfast and Lunch
Drink another 16 ounce glass of Hunter Wellness Mojo Juice if you are hungry. Or you can just snack on raw vegetables.

Lunch
Mixed green salad including fresh beets topped with olive oil and balsamic vinegar.

Mid-Afternoon
Drink 16 ounces of Hunter Wellness Mojo Juice.

Dinner
Steamed vegetables (not steamed over 3 minutes).

Before Bed
Relax with a cup of caffeine free tea.

Follow this program as closely as possible for a minimum of three days to really see the results. If you are hungry at any point in this program munch on the Hunter Wellness Snack Bag (get a gallon zip lock bag and fill it with sliced cucumber; cherry tomatoes; cut up green, red, orange, yellow peppers; carrots; broccoli; celery; etc.)

Along with the detoxification program outlined above, all of the suggestions below will aid in the body's natural detoxification processes and also boost your mood and energy levels. Try some of the options listed below during your cleanse and you will feel so good that you will want to incorporate them in your life on a regular basis.

- Take a 30 minute walk.
- Go for a 30 minute swim.
- Use the sauna or steam room to increase circulation and assist the elimination process through the skin.
- Take three deep breaths every hour to the following ratio: Inhale for a count of six, hold.
  For, four counts and exhale for a count of eight (using your diaphragm so your stomach sticks out as you inhale). As you exhale visualize the exhale to be a detoxifying breath.
- Before you hop in the shower do five minutes of skin brushing with a boar hair brush for your whole body. This increases circulation and helps break down fatty deposits.
- Get a massage.
- Take a bath and exfoliate with bath salts.
- Treat every day as if it is the last day of your life.
- Engage in positive thoughts to make you feel good.
- Hang out with positive people.

- Let go of the past.
- Treat yourself with respect and be authentic.
- Learn the difference between who you are and what others think about you.
- Be respectful to your environment.
- Be respectful to your neighbors and practice kindness to everyone.

Step Two
Purify Your Negative Emotions

I believe that many major illnesses, injury and drama are caused by stress. 100% of stress is caused by the way you react mentally and emotionally to life. There are thousands of negative thoughts racing through your brain on a daily basis, and you have the power and the ability to control them.

In order to purify our negative emotions we need to change our attitude. Our thoughts and feelings are the driving force to our actions and attitudes. If I continued to feel dumb and not good enough, I would have never made it through college, and I definitely would not be writing this book.

We all know that we have many thoughts, some good for us, and some very demanding based on the beliefs that we have accumulated during our life.

Pick a list of good feelings and thoughts you want to have and find ways to experience them daily. Make a list of things that make you happy and go over that list every day and count your blessings.

You know that you are like the people whom you hang around with? There is a great proverb which says, "Tell me who your friends are and I will tell you who you are". So what about you? Are you around people who drag you down? Do you drag other people down?

Toxic people can also take a toll on your health, especially people who always take and never give, or people who say they love you but are judging you. A part of my healing journey was to "divorce" the people in my life that were not supporting who I was, or were not giving but only taking. When I decided that I was most comfortable being a lesbian, I had friends and family tell me, "I will always love you, but not your sin." "Love the person, hate the sin."

I also had "friends" that would never meet me half way; it was always about them. In order to maintain being their friend, I would have to do all the work.

Do the people in your life encourage you and build you up? Are they a good influence on you in terms of healthy living and eating habits? If not, perhaps it is time to begin seeking out others that are more like-minded; those who understand the importance of mutually beneficial relationships that feed into each other, rather than emotionally drain each other.

It is important to spend time with positive people so that you are sharing yourself with people that do not judge and who are accepting and supportive of your personal growth.

It is important to stay away from negative people no matter who they are. Negative people criticize and complain and blame others for their problems. They are infectious, and in time, you will adopt their attitude if you hang around them for a long period of time. Now we need to learn to control the inner thoughts that go on in our minds. You need to know what triggers your negative thoughts and emotions.

Keep in mind that it is never the actual event or situation that makes you feel bad, but your perception. Not only can your thoughts distort reality, but they can also distort your feelings. Here is an example:

You are not invited to a party you think you should have been invited to.

You might think:
- I did something wrong
- I am not a priority
- I am not important
- I am not worthy

So then you start feeling:
- Angry
- Hurt
- Worthless
- Inadequate

The reality is the person forgot to invite you, and several other people, because he/she was distracted.

Remember that nothing in life has meaning unless you give it meaning.

It is important to learn to control your inner voice so that you do not become toxic.

Your inner dialog is very damaging to your spirit if you are being negative. It is important to remember that it is not the trigger that makes your mind become toxic. What you say to yourself and what meaning you give it is what causes your pain.

Here are five helpful steps I learned in my psychology classes and have applied to my life. You can use them as a quick reference to keep your toxic emotions in check.

1. Assuming
When you assume, you are usually assuming the worst, you don't have all the facts. It is important to test the assumption so that you know the truth. It is your responsibility to get proof so that you do not put yourself in a toxic mode.

For years, I assumed that God would not love me because I was not abiding by the church rules. I realized that my assumption was not correct, that I was perfect in the sight of God, and that being me was not a sin.

2. Labeling
When you are labeling yourself you are allowing yourself and others to describe who you are.

For example:
- I am always sick
- I am ugly
- I am a loser
- I am stupid
- I am a sinner

It is important to stop labeling yourself and be more specific of your thoughts.

Never allow someone to label you in a negative way.

Instead of saying "I am a loser" say "That did not work out how I would have liked."

Instead of saying "I am a sinner" say "I should get curious as to why I believe in such limited beliefs."

Remember, if we did not have negative labels separating us, we would all be the same. If you lined up 300 people, none of them would be like you. You are unique and wonderful and one of a kind. Besides, negative labels simply give people reasons to discriminate.

If you focus on positive labels you will empower your life with strength beyond your imagination.

3. Blaming
Do you blame others instead of accepting responsibility for the outcomes that don't go your way?

Do you say?
- If only my parents would have………..
- It's your fault I am fat.
- I did it because you made me so mad.
- You always…………………..

Get out of victim mode. You are responsible for ALL of your actions.

You are not helpless and you CAN do ANYTHING you set your mind to.

Everything has an effect on you, and at the end of the day, you have the responsibility to let it affect you or not. Don't make excuses when you are responsible for the way you feel.

Take ownership, it's your body, your life, your emotions, your reactions. Deal with it!

4. Personalizing
Personalizing is the opposite of blaming.
With personalizing:
- It's my fault my daughter is not career-minded.
- If I wasn't so needy, I would have more friends.
- It's my fault we got divorced.

It is important to remember not to blame yourself because it always takes two for an event to happen. You might have had influence, but at the end of the day we all make our own decisions. Your opinion is probably one of hundreds of opinions, and in all honesty, you might need to humble your thoughts, because none of us have that much power.

5. Should-Would-Could
Do you always say to yourself "I should be this" or "I should do that"?
- I should be happy.
- I would have had more money by now.
- I could have had more friends.
- I would be thinner.

These are demands that you place upon yourself. Ask yourself why you are not doing something you "should" do? What is stopping you? What is the worst thing that could happen to you if you did not reach your goal?

Stop setting yourself up for failure and start doing what you say. It's that simple.

By focusing on should-would-could you are making yourself feel inadequate and hopeless.

Try changing your should-would-could to "I will".

When you feel negative thoughts, or if you feel someone is attacking you, it may be a reflection of your own behavior.

Be honest with yourself and if you are ready, take responsibility for your behavior by journaling your emotions so that you have clarity, and clear any toxic thoughts you have harbored.

Step Three
Nourish your Body with Healthy Foods

If you want to be healthy you need to understand and know your body's need for fuel. It is not about being on a diet with rules and restrictions nor is it about eating what you want. Dieting will put your body through periods of stress and is a never ending cycle of failure. Jumping from one diet to the other is sabotaging your goals to become healthy because your body is not meant to internally be on a rollercoaster ride. Nor can your body handle being bombarded with junk food and toxins that create chronic illnesses. My Food Plan is learning the basics of nutrition so that you can avoid risks of illness. Eating to Live is about learning all the avenues to empower your life by making the right food choices. Most importantly, you want to eat in order to feel good, to feel balanced and become a healthier you.

The longer you are on this food plan, the more closely you follow it, the easier it will be to stick to it. Your cravings for processed foods and sugar will actually diminish. Old habits are hard to break, so take your time in changing your nutritional habits so you don't slip back into your old way of eating.

Remember that your body is your temple, and what you eat will either nourish or deplete the cells and organs that are working hard at giving you a healthy life. Before you eat, be mindful of why and what you are eating. Make sure it is for fuel and not because of toxic emotions!

This might be a good time to clean out your refrigerator, freezer and food cabinet. Get rid of EVERYTHING that will tempt you or sabotage your road to health.

The food plan that I am providing you with is what helped me heal from Chronic Fatigue. I also give this to all my clients that suffer from auto immune diseases.

Food Plan

Proteins
Eat small amounts of proteins; both animal and vegetarian sources of protein are beneficial as long as they are organic. Organic eggs are also an excellent source of protein. My approach is whole food nutrition so eat the whole egg! Avoid frying your proteins: Gas grilled, boiled, steamed, soft boiled, or poached is best.

Vegetables
Eat as much as you want, but "do" eat, as it is VERY IMPORTANT not to skip eating your vegetables. Always look for a variety in color, although make the green leafy type your preference. This includes spinach, chard, beet greens, kale, broccoli, mustard and collard greens. Try to buy fresh organic as much as possible. Do not eat canned vegetables, raw is the better choice.

Fruits
Please do not drink your fruits. Fruit juice is loaded with the simple sugar fructose, which is diverted into forming triglycerides and ultimately stored as fat. Without the fiber in the fruit, juice sends a rapid burst of sugar into the blood stream. When you do eat fruit, only eat one type of fruit at a time on an empty stomach.

Wheat and Grains
Minimize all grains. Brown rice, quinoa, amaranth and millet should be your only choices. Allow yourself ONLY One Serving per day.

Sweeteners
Use only a small amount of raw organic honey or Stevia as sweetener. Absolutely NO corn syrup, table sugar or artificial sweeteners.

Fats
Use olive oil (cold pressed, extra virgin), coconut oil, flax seed and grape seed oils. These are all actually beneficial, as long as they are cold-pressed. When cooking use only raw butter and coconut oil as they are safe to cook with on high heat. Avoid all hydrogenated and partially hydrogenated fats such as margarine. They are poisons to your temple.

Milk Products
Avoiding dairy will make it much easier for you to attain your optimal level of health and hormonal balance. Raw goat and sheep cheeses and goat milk products are great alternatives.

Liquids
Water is best. Your weight divided in half is how many ounces of water you should have per day. You may also have herbal tea. Avoid all soda. Fruit juices are not healthy choices because of their high fructose content and dumping of sugar into the blood stream.

If you enjoy wine or beer and still insist, there are some guidelines. Red wine has less sugar than white wines. Good quality beer is the best. Usually foreign beers are made with better quality ingredients.

Avoid junk food, processed food and sweets! It is impossible to balance your body's chemistry when eating these foods. The more carbohydrates you eat the more you will crave them. It is a vicious cycle that never ends.

Eating a smaller amount reduces the stress of digestion on your energy supply. Eating small meals conserves energy. Give your body's energy a chance to keep up with digestion by not overwhelming it with large portions. When digestion is impaired, yeast overgrowth, gas, inflammation, food reactions and sugar imbalances are the result.

Here are 10 tips for healthy digestion:
1. Eat in a non stressed environment.
2. Rest after your meal.
3. Always sit while eating.
4. Do not eat when you are upset.
5. Avoid overeating.
6. Do not drink while you eat (avoid cold drinks).
7. Eat at a moderate pace.
8. Do not eat until your previous meal has been digested.
9. Do not overcook your food.
10. Do not eat when you are upset.

Self Honor Mantra

I am the temple for my divine.
I am a yielded vessel, a tabernacle,
a dwelling place for my great spirit.
I will honor my body, mind and spirit
and protect it with sacred living.
I am one with God and the universe
therefore it is my responsibility to take care of me.

Chapter Eleven
living in the moment what is your focus?

I Am Blessed

As an adult, this lesson was hard for me, because I was always having inner thoughts in my head that were toxic. I needed to be a busy body in everyone's life so that I was liked and needed. When I learned to let go and live in the moment, and focus on my wants, needs and desires, I started feeling less burdened and full of joy. Try treating each day as if it were your last day on earth.

Don't look back on your past; its already gone so why are you dwelling on it... get over it! I now practice what I call 'The Art of Deleting.' Sometimes we dwell on things in the past so we can keep holding on to things that no longer serve us. Holding on to those bad feelings is not going to change the past or change the other person or event. Don't become a vessel of those toxic thoughts. Learn to put them behind you by just hitting your "DELETE" button.

Accept what you cannot change and change what you can with love, and be mindful of the difference between the two. Don't dwell on your future to the point where you forget about your now, because you are not promised anything past this moment.

You must live your life in the moment as if you were a child at a birthday party. The child has no worries or cares but is just living in the moment. So whatever you are doing, live it in the moment and add joy to your mindset. When this happens you become spontaneous, which helps you to live with whatever is happing in your life. I am not saying forget your responsibilities, just simply live in the moment and be clear on your goals. What is your focus?

What goals do you want to accomplish today? What goals do you want to accomplish this week?

Making sure you have healthy goals; working towards those goals while living in the moment can be very rewarding. You will feel accomplished and liberated at the same time.

Here is an example:
1. You can choose to work all day with zero brakes and only focus on your duties.
2. Or, you can choose to accomplish your goals, take free time for yourself, being mindful of everything around you so that you don't miss out on all the beautiful miracles surrounding your life.

Leading a happy and successful life requires us to make healthy choices, think positively, and believe in ourselves. Taking the wrong action or taking no action leaves us frustrated, feeling powerless, hopeless and stuck. When we change our thoughts we change our lives. If our thinking is negative the outcome is negative. When we think positive the outcome is positive.

Instead of focusing on things we can't control it's important to identify and change the things we can, so that we can live in the moment. Here are some ideas to focus on so that you can live in the moment.

Nourish Your Mind
- Replace negative thoughts and beliefs with positive ones.
- Open up. Talk about your problems with someone you trust.
- Write out your problems in a journal.
- Think before you speak.
- Avoid worry and anxiety. Breathe deeply.
- Get at least seven hours of sleep.
- Watch little or no TV.
- Refuse to gossip or engage in negative talk.
- Be patient.
- Use daily affirmations.

Be Active
- Learn to love exercising.
- Play outside.
- Walk, ski, rollerblade, hike, swim, run.
- Practice yoga/pilates.
- Do something unpredictable.

Take Care of Your Temple
- Understand your body.
- Eat less and eat healthy.
- Drink plenty of water.
- Pay attention to your body.
- Try a new fruit or vegetable each week.
- Floss and brush your teeth regularly.
- Wash your hands regularly.
- Eliminate junk food.
- Do a detoxification program.

Pamper Yourself
- Visit a spa.
- Get a manicure & pedicure.
- Get a Massage.
- Learn to enjoy your own company.
- Write a love letter to yourself.
- Burn candles and relax.

Live in the Moment
- Take time out.
- Read.
- Dance.
- Play games.
- Listen to music.
- Spend time with friends.
- Grow a garden.

- Ride your bike.
- Do scrapbooking.
- Find a new hobby.
- Appreciate yourself.
- Take a nature walk
- Be more social.
- Volunteer.

Eliminate Stress
- Eat healthy.
- Focus on best case scenarios.
- Stop whining and complaining.
- Don't compare yourself to others.
- Replace negative thoughts with positive thoughts.
- Let go of toxic people.
- Learn to meditate.
- Let go of trivial things.
- Don't take things personally.
- Ask for what you want.
- Love yourself.
- Cut clutter.
- Detoxify your calendar.

I Am Blessed Mantra

I am blessed by the beauty that is around me.
I am thankful for the gifts in my life.
Every breath that I take is a miracle
and I will be mindful in making sure each moment
is spent in love and laughter.
In doing this I will grow and become all that I am
and all that I desire.
I am truly thankful for my life!

Chapter Twelve
living by your virtues

Organic Love

A virtue is a habit or quality that allows us to succeed with a purpose. A virtue is a moral excellence, a positive trait or quality deemed to be morally good, which makes virtues valuable as a foundation for principles.

Having personal virtues promotes collective and individual greatness. Living by virtues that I believe in and virtues that are positive helps me to live my life with integrity. They help me build my spiritual habits into every day actions that I can be proud of. In this chapter, there are more than 300 virtues listed.

Life presents us, at every moment, with opportunities to practice the Virtues: How you choose to act or respond to what presents itself to you. Here are suggestions for practicing them more consciously:

- Make a list and circle the virtues you want to practice at the beginning of each week. Post them visibly so you are reminded of them every day.

- Create a set of "Virtue Cards" and pick one each day to practice.

- Look up in a dictionary any words that are unfamiliar, or which you can't define, including the derivation, usage, and examples.

- Meditate on one virtue each day.

My Virtues

a
ability
abundance
acceptance
accountability
accuracy
achievement
acknowledgement
activism
adaptability
adoration
adventure
advice
affection
aging gracefully
allowing
altruism
amazement
ambition
anticipation
apology
appeasement
appreciation
appreciation of beauty
 appreciation of excellence
approbation
appropriate knowledge
appropriate conduct
approval
art
assertiveness
assumptions
atonement
attention
attitude
austerity
authenticity
authority
autonomy
awareness
awe

b
balance
beauty
being true to oneself
belief
benevolence
benignity
bliss
bravery

c
candor
capacity to love
capacity to be loved
care
caring
caution
celebration
celibacy
certainty
chance
change
character
charity
charm
chastity
cheerfulness
chivalry
choice
citizenship
civility
clarity
class
cleanliness
coincidence
collaboration
commitment
communication
communion
community
companionship
compassion
completeness
composure
comprehension
compromise
concentration
confession
confidence
congruence
conscience
consciousness
consecration
consideration
consistency
contemplation
contentment
contribution
control
conviction
cooperation
cooperativeness
correctness
courage
courteousness
courtesy

creativity
credibility
critical thinking
culture
curiosity

d

death (acceptance of)
decency
dedication
deliberation
delight
dependability
desire
destiny
detachment
determination
devotion to virtues
devotion to others
dignity
diligence
diplomacy
discernment
discipline
dis-creation
 (of what is no
 longer needed)
discretion
disillusion
dissolution
diversity
dreams
dutifulness

e

eagerness
extravagance
earnestness
ecstasy

education
efficiency
endurance
effort
 (doing one's
 best)
elegance
elevation
eloquence
emotion
empathy
encouragement
endurance
energy
enlightenment
enthusiasm
epiphany
equality
equanimity
esteem
etiquette
excellence
excitement
expressiveness

f

failure
 (allowing for)
fairness
faith
faithfulness
family
fearlessness
feeling
fidelity
finishing what's
 started
flexibility
flow
focus

forbearance
foresight
forgiveness
fortitude
frankness
freedom
friendliness
friendship
frugality
fulfillment
fun

g

gallantry
generosity
genius
gentleness
genuineness
glory
goals
godliness
good speech
goodness
grace
grandeur
gratefulness
gratitude
gravitas
gravity
growth

h

happiness
harmlessness
harmony
healing
health
heaven on earth
helpfulness
helping others

holiness
honesty
honor
hope
hopefulness
hospitality
humanity
humility
humor

i
idealism
ideals
identities (ease of shifting)
illumination
imagination
impartiality
imperfection (allowing for)
inclusion
incorruptibility
independence
individuality
industriousness
ingenuity
initiative
inner exploration
innocence
innovation
insight
inspiration
instinct
integrity
intelligence
interdependence
interest in the world
intimacy
intuition

inventiveness
investigation
irony

j
joy
joyfulness
judgment (good)
justice

k
kind speech
kindness
kinship
knowledge

l
laughter
leadership
learning
leisure
liberalism
liberty
listening
logic
love

m
majesty
management
manners
maturity
meaning
mellowness
mercy
mildness
mindfulness
mistakes (allowing for)
moderation

modesty
morality
motivation

n
niceness
nobility
non-covetousness
non-duality
non-separateness
non-violence
nostalgia
nurturance
nurturing

o
obedience (to higher principles)
objectivity
obligations (fulfillment of)
open-heartedness
open-mindedness
openness
optimism
order
orderliness
organization
originality
overcoming adversity (& impediments)

p
pacifism
paradise
passion
patience
patriotism

peace
peacefulness
penitence
pensiveness
perseverance
persistence
personality
perspective
persuasion
philanthropy
piety
pity
planning
play
playfulness
pleasure
pluralism
politeness
positive bias
potency
potential
power (right use of)
practice
practicality
pragmatism
praise
prayer
prayerfulness
precision
principles
privacy
privilege
potency
probity
problem-solving
productivity
professionalism
profit
promises
propriety

prosperity
protection
protest
prudence
punctuality
purification
purity
purity of heart
purpose
purposeful work
purposefulness

q
quality evaluation
quality improvement
Quest

r
radiance
rapture
rationality
realism
reality
realization
reason
rebirth
receptivity
reciprocity
reconciliation
rectitude
redemption
refinement
reflection
relaxation
release
reliability
religiosity
remembering
remembrance
remorse

renunciation
repentance
reputation
research
resilience
resisting temptations
resolution
respect
respectability
respectfulness
responsibility
restraint
reverence
right action
right concentration
right effort
right intention
right livelihood
right mindfulness
right speech
right use of power
right use of will
righteousness
rights (respect for)
risk taking
rituals
romance
roots

s
sacredness
sacrifice
sadness
sanity
satiety
satisfaction
secrecy (proper use)
security
seeing
self-awareness

self-confidence
self-control
self-discipline
self-esteem
self-examination
self-expression
self-improvement
self-possession
self-regulation
self-reliance
self-respect
self-restraint
self-righteousness
self-trust
sense of purpose
sensibility
sensitivity
sensory pleasure
sensuality
sentimentality
serendipity
serenity
service
sharing
silence
simplicity
sincerity
skepticism
skill
smartness
sobriety
social intelligence
social responsibility
solidarity
social intelligence
social responsibility
solidarity
solitude
soul evolution
soulfulness

spirit
spiritual insight
spirituality
sportsmanship
steadfastness
stick-to-it-iveness
straightforwardness
strength
stress ("good")
study
success
succor
suffering (with understanding)
support of others
surrender
sweet-tempered
sympathy
synergy

t

tact
tactfulness
talent
taste
teamwork
temperance
tenacity
tenderness
thankfulness
thoughtfulness
thoroughness
thrift
tolerance
tranquility
training
transcendence
transformation
transition
trust

trustworthiness
truthfulness

u

unconditional love
understanding
unity
universality
unselfishness

v

valor
values
victory
vigor
virility
vision
vitality
vulnerability

w

wealth
wholesomeness
will
wisdom
wonder
work
worship
worth

y

youthfulness

z

zealousness
zest

Organic Love Mantra

Every day I will strive to challenge my heart
to live a worthy life.
My expressions and actions will be positive
and only manifest good seeds of love and light.
I will let go of any ego that gets in the way
of pure organic love.

Chapter Thirteen
souful freedom organically born again

I Am

For 30 years I held on to personal values and spiritual beliefs that did not support my true self. I followed personal and spiritual rules that hindered my growth. I lived in FEAR, because of limiting beliefs about my spiritual afterlife and how I thought God viewed me. I have been saved and I have been born again by religious standards, and none of it gave me the peace and empowerment to be authentically me.

It wasn't until I decided to get curious about why I believed what I believed, and to actually challenge those beliefs, that I became aware of the real truth for me. When I gave myself permission to change my thoughts and when I took the step of courage to be me and not what I thought I was "supposed to be," I found real freedom, Soul Freedom®.

When I started redefining my spiritual beliefs in a structure that was of higher vibration rather than judgment or condemnation, I started feeling complete joy and peace in my life. I had to let go of the God that was branded or labeled to suit a certain denomination and I had to realize that my road to God was not like any other. It was personal. I sought out my own salvation and I now have a personal relationship with MY God.

I had to be Organically Born Again; to be of a pure heart and define God by my own authenticity, to be free from toxic emotions and the low vibration of judgment, fear, anger, doubt, jealously and hate.

The more I lived by the standards that were authentic to me the more I developed a relationship with MY GOD and the more I experienced Soulful Freedom®.

My hope for you is that you feel perfect in your skin. If you don't feel perfect in your skin, then get curious and make some changes in your life by:

- Redefining your values
- Redefining your beliefs
- Attacking your fear
- Changing your rules
- Embracing your new spirituality
- Taking care of your temple
- Living your new life

Don't forget that you are a beautiful soul, deserving of all the love and joy your heart can hold. You are worthy of being empowered with courage, and that you can have and experience your wants, needs and desires. Don't allow ANYONE to tell you otherwise. Step into your reality and embrace who you really are. God created you and you are already perfect in the presence of the Divine. Allow your life to be precious and meaningful with values and beliefs that are your own. Allow yourself to create rules that help you to grow personally and spiritually. Trust in YOUR GOD to give you guidance and understanding about the most important matters of your heart.

I challenge you to allow yourself to be Organically Born Again so that you can feel Soulful Freedom®.

I Am Mantra

I Am a Spiritual vessel
for the pure light of the Great Spirit.
I Am a sacred temple
that holds the breath of the Divine.
I Am creativity and strength
that can move mountains.
I Am one with my values.
I Am one with my beliefs.
I Am truth.
I Am perfect in the sight of God.
I Am perfect in Me!

about the author

MaryLou Hunter, HHP, has been helping her clients improve the quality of their lives for 20 years. As an intuitive energy healer, she specializes in spiritual mind/body connections in regards to healing. Her expertise in bodywork with her knowledge of energy and nutrition offers a complete coaching experience.

MaryLou is a Holistic Health Practitioner, Certified Nutrition and Life Coach, Reiki Master Teacher, Shamanic Counselor and Ordained Minister. She continues her education and will obtain her Doctorate Degree in Holistic Life Coaching in Spring of 2014.

Her goals are to educate the basics of life balance. Her mission is to bring back the simplicity of health through natural means of nutrition and healing the soul by focusing on the emotional toxicities that have been created by living an unbalanced life. Her passion in life is helping people get back to the first step to healing, which is to love yourself unconditionally. Once you understand that, you will begin to experience Soulful Freedom®.

www.ingramcontent.com/pod-product-compliance
Lightning Source LLC
Chambersburg PA
CBHW070200100426
42743CB00013B/2982